The Low Density LIFESTYLE

The Low Density LIFESTYLE

The Secret to Becoming FREE

Michael Wayne

iThink Books

The Low Density Lifestyle: The Secret to Becoming FREE

www.lowdensitylifestyle.com

Copyright© 2011 Michael Wayne

All rights reserved. No part of this book may be reproduced or transmitted in any form or by any means, electronic or mechanical, including photocopying, recording, or by any other information storage and retrieval system, without written permission from the publisher, except for the inclusion of brief quotations in a review.

ISBN-13: 978-0-9766797-2-1
ISBN-10: 0-9766797-2-8

Published by iThink Books
P.O. Box 393
Saratoga Springs, NY 12866
iThinkBooks@me.com

Interior and Cover design by BeanTree Designs
beantreedesigns@aol.com

Table of Contents

Introduction ... 7

Part I:
Low and High Density

1: What is a Low Density Lifestyle? ... 11
2: Low Density vs. High Density Lifestyle ... 19
3: How Did We Get Here? ... 25

Part II:
How to Achieve a Low Density Lifestyle:
A 12-Step Guide to Becoming FREE

4: Diet and Nutrition ... 31
5: Health and Wellness ... 37
6: Movement and Exercise ... 41
7: Flexibility of Body and Mind ... 47
8: Mindfulness ... 51
9: Integrity ... 59
10: Attitude and Emotions ... 63

11:	Abundance	69
12:	Laughter	73
13:	The Dreamer	77
14:	Do What You Love	87
15:	Connecting to the Spiritual Dimension	93

Part III:
Impediments to Living a Low Density Lifestyle

16:	Stress	99
17:	Dogma	105
18:	Resistance to New Ideas	111
19:	Control and Fear	119
20:	Poor Diet, Poor Health	127
21:	The Curse of Knowledge	129

Part IV:
What a Low Density Lifestyle Can Do For You

22:	Health and Longevity	137
23:	Happiness and Joy	143
24:	Better Relationships, Better Sex	147
25:	Focus and Clarity of Thought	153
26:	Creativity and Genius	157
27:	Productivity and Success	161
28:	Intuition	165
29:	Inner Peace	167
30:	Enlightenment	169

Conclusion:
Being Bold, Touching Your Greatness   171

Introduction

This is a book about many things—health, wellness, happiness, fulfillment, doing what you love, movement, being a creative thinker—but at the same time, it's about one thing: living to your maximum potential.

Living to your maximum potential means feeding, cultivating and developing your body, mind, emotions, and spirit. And to do so, there are a number of steps to be taken. But they are all interconnected and all related; since we are integrated beings, with a unison of body, mind, emotions and spirit, it makes sense that feeding one aspect of who we are feeds other aspects.

My goal with this book is to help you become more complete human beings. We are meant to live a conscious life, a more awakened life, and this means being complete human beings.

What do I mean by a complete human being? I define that as someone who is physically healthy; in touch and aware and mindful of their emotions and not prone to becoming reactive with others; capable of holding complex thoughts in their head and maintaining the knowledge that ideas, problems and solutions are rarely black and white, and generally tend towards the subtle shades of grey; and have a connection to the spiritual dimension of life.

I call this approach a Low Density Lifestyle, and I consider it a model for living. In the ensuing pages I explain what I mean by this and how you can achieve it. But you can call this approach to life by any other name; my aim is to give it a name that is easy to grasp and understand, and by doing so, make it easier to attain.

I hope you find it easy to attain, and it helps set you on the path towards health, happiness, fulfillment, and even enlightenment.

Part I:
Low and High Density

1

What is a Low Density Lifestyle?

The universe operates through dynamic exchange...giving and receiving are different aspects of the flow of energy in the universe. And in our willingness to give that which we seek, we keep the abundance of the universe circulating in our lives.
– Deepak Chopra

"Well," said Pooh, "what I like best," and then he had to stop and think. Because although Eating Honey was a very good thing to do, there was a moment just before you began to eat it which was better than when you were, but he didn't know what it was called.
– A.A. Milne

"Total control" of one's own mind is in fact too strong an expression to describe accurately what happens when one is in flow. The point is not that one can always do what one wants, but rather that the possibility of making things happen as one wishes is present in a way that seldom occurs in "real" life.
– Mihaly Csikszentmihalyi

What is a Low Density Lifestyle? It is experiencing and living in a more relaxed, less stressed, and calm, clear and focused manner on an everyday basis. It is also a way that can lead you to better health and happiness, along with living a more fulfilled life.

Would you like to feel healthier and have a greater sense of well-being? Feel happier, more joy and passion, and a greater sense of fulfillment? Have better relationships with your family, friends and significant other? Have an enhanced sex life? Improve your performance in your work, life and play? Gain complete self-mastery over your thoughts, feelings, and actions? Use more of your potential? Feel complete inner peace?

All this and more is what a Low Density Lifestyle can do for you.

Achieving this state is not hard, although for so many people there are countless roadblocks, most of which are self-inflicted. But when you arrive there you know it, because suddenly you begin to feel that everything flows and all tasks are done effortlessly. In this situation, the body and mind are in such resonance that you feel like you are "in the zone."

A Low Density Lifestyle is the antidote for our increasingly fast-paced lifestyle. With each passing day our hectic existence is becoming more and more unbalanced and out of control. The pace of our society is leading us to the complete opposite of a Low Density Lifestyle—to a High Density Lifestyle. Collectively, all of us have been affected and are literally crying for a pause, a virtual time-out from this torrid pace.

When you are living a Low Density Lifestyle, you have less density and rigidity in the body—this means there are fewer blockages that can obstruct the dynamic flow of energy that circulates throughout the body and mind.

Our natural inclination is to aspire towards a flow state, no matter the obstacles, because intuitively we know that this is the true path to happiness, health, inner peace, success, productivity, focus, clarity and quality of thought, better relationships, love and spiritual growth. We all want to be there, yet we don't know how, nor do we have a clear road map as a guide.

All of us have caught a peek, even if it is glimpsing, of what a Low Density Lifestyle is like. We all have been there. Perhaps it was when you were on vacation, or when you did something you felt passionate about. Maybe it's been when you were absorbed in nature; it could even have been when you were in the middle of a crowded city street. Time and place aren't necessarily the key factors in achieving a Low Density Lifestyle, because ultimately it's a state of mind.

When you live a Low Density Lifestyle, you are more fluid and flexible of body and mind, and less inflexible, rigid and uncompromising. Fluidity of body and mind doesn't just mean that you can twist yourself into a pretzel, as some yoga practitioners are able to do (and if you can't do that, it doesn't mean you are not capable of living a Low Density Lifestyle). Instead, being fluid of body and mind means having a certain flexibility of the body, within the limitations you may have, and an equally important fluidity of the mind— your thinking is flexible, and you don't hold onto belief patterns if they are not viable.

Thoughts are energy, and if your thought patterns are unyielding and inflexible, it brings a certain degree of density into your body and mind, making it harder to achieve the Low Density Lifestyle.

Paulo Coelho, author of *The Alchemist*, said, "Be like the fountain that overflows, not like the cistern that merely contains." In essence, this is the formula for living a Low Density Lifestyle. If you let go of your densities and rigidities, and overcome your blockages, you will be like a fountain. You then become a circuit of energy, flowing infinitely, much like an unimpeded electrical circuit in which the electricity freely courses throughout.

But if you become a slave to your blockages, you become more like a cistern, and things begin to boil up on the inside, like a pent-up pressure cooker. If this continues on a regular basis, the obstructions in the body become denser and more impenetrable.

Some people object to the concept of a Low Density Lifestyle because they feel that to get ahead in this world means to push forward and be aggressive and assertive. They equate a Low Density Lifestyle as one in which you are too chilled out and mellow to take an active part in this competitive world.

But nothing can be further from the truth. Living a Low Density Lifestyle doesn't mean that you completely "check-out" of life, or just "bliss out." This is just not a reality, especially in our fast-paced times. Instead, it means that you live in a continual state of flow. This is what most athletes call being in the zone: everything just seems to go your way. And athletes will be the first to tell you that when they are in the flow state, they perform at higher levels.

Shawn Phillips, the well-known athlete, bodybuilder and author of *Strength for Life*, had this to say about the subject:

> From the beginning, what I was connecting with in the gym was a universal energy source. I would just feel it flowing. Even when I was twenty years old, I called the gym my church. When I was there, it wasn't about being social; it was about doing my practice. I was in it. I was in the zone.

The same can be said for all other walks of life: when you are in a flow state and living a Low Density Lifestyle, you will be more successful, healthier and happier. Your thinking processes will be clearer and you will use more of your latent potential.

The ancient Chinese philosophers called this wu wei, or effortless effort. The state of effortless effort describes a condition in which you are busy with effort, yet it seems effortless, as if the world seems to be working for you. You feel calm yet alert, focused yet receptive, drawing force from the storm while standing in its eye, acutely using all your senses. Like a marathoner who feels pulled forward, you accomplish the most with a minimum of energy. In this state hard work does not feel like work at all.

When you are in the state of effortless effort, you can labor for hours on end, at times functioning on little sleep, and yet feel full of energy and life. You are firing on all cylinders, and the universe seems like a giant playground.

Unfortunately, we don't achieve the state of effortless effort—where we are tapping into the greater part of our potential—too often, if ever. Scientists say that at most we use five percent of our potential, although there are some researchers who downgrade the number to just one percent.

The reason we use so little is that as the densities in the body become more rigid, they obstruct the free flow of circulating energy, and by doing so they block information that the body and mind convey to each other and receive from external sources.

This is no different than the theory of electricity. Electrical current flows through the path of least resistance, as does your life force. When the body is in a high density environment, the life force cannot flow well, because of the increased resistance.

The body and mind are like satellite dishes, and can pick up signals from both internal and external sources. The signals received that originate from internal sources are communications that the body and mind transmit to one another in the form of thoughts and ideas. The signals that derive from external sources are communications (in the form of wavelengths) that emanate from the universe and the vast unlimited field of infinite energy, called the Zero-Point Field.

The science of consciousness tells us that not only is there a singular consciousness—the thought processes within us—but there is also a universal consciousness—thought processes that stem from what is called the Quantum Vacuum, or Zero-Point Field. This field is where all matter, energy and consciousness originate.

All life and energy begin, according to theoretical physics, in an endless and boundless primal soup known as the Zero-Point Field. This field, which pervades the entire universe and teems with infinite amounts of information, consciousness and energy, has a direct pipeline to our body and mind.

Have you ever experienced the Aha moment, that magical flash when the light bulb goes off in your head and you have an epiphany? Everyone has had this happen at one time or another; it is an instance when you suddenly have focused clarity. The results from this might be a brilliant idea, a moment of lucidity about a difficult situation you are in, or some other valuable insight. The Aha moment is a communication from the Zero-Point Field, directly picked up by the body's satellite dish.

The ability to tap into the Zero-Point Field can lead to accessing a larger whole where greater potentials exist. When you are able to come into contact with your greater potential, you feel more alive, vibrant, alert, healthier, happier, focused, and you also think in a more holistic manner—in other words, you are living a Low Density Lifestyle.

This is the penultimate (although not the only) result of being fluid of body and mind and living a Low Density Lifestyle—the ability to fully and completely live up to your innate potential.

Being able to do this may not happen overnight, but given time, and the desire to achieve the natural aspirations of body and mind, you can live a Low Density Lifestyle.

Remember, it is not hard to achieve this state, although it takes work. In Part II of this book, you will find a twelve-step guide to help steer you in the right direction. But in actuality, there really are only a couple of key components. One is to experience flow. Another is to practice effortless effort. And one other is to relax, slow down and let go.

There is a Spanish saying, "Cuán hermoso es de no hacer nada, y entonces descansar después." This wise traditional proverb translates as, "How beautiful it is to do nothing, and then to rest afterward."

And Leonardo da Vinci said, "Every now and then go away, have a little relaxation, for when you come back to your work your judgment will be surer. Go some distance away because then the work appears smaller and more of it can be taken in at a glance and a lack of harmony and proportion is more readily seen."

It is when you practice these essential characteristics—flow, relax and effortless effort—that you promote a Low Density Lifestyle. An easy way to make these a part of your life is to commit to memory the simple formula: LDL = FREE.

That prescription stands for Low Density Lifestyle = Flow/Relax/Effortless Effort. Keep that in mind: to get away from a High Density Lifestyle, you just have to practice being FREE.

2

Low Density vs. High Density Lifestyle

If you ask what is the single most important key to longevity, I would have to say it is avoiding worry, stress and tension. And if you didn't ask me, I'd still have to say it.
— George Burns

Half our life is spent trying to find something to do with the time we have rushed through life trying to save.
— Will Rogers

There is more to life than increasing its speed.
— Mohandas K. Gandhi

10 Signs That You're Leading a High-Density Lifestyle

1. That mother and her 3-year old just don't seem to walk fast enough through the crosswalk for you!

2. You begin to think that there is a conspiracy out there to make you late for work every single morning!

3. You're starting a petition to replace food, water and air as our basic needs with an extra large coffee with triple cream and triple sugar.

4. When you leave the driveway in the morning it looks like a chase scene from your favorite police show.

5. The space around your lounge chair at your kid's soccer, hockey or baseball games look like the desk at your office.

6. You pray for red lights because you figure that waiting at the light is a great time to get some business done.

7. You find sitting anywhere for beyond five minutes is a great time to get into REM state.

8. You've developed your own system of increasing muscle tone in your neck and shoulders without the benefits of working out!

9. You have discovered that ten minutes a day of crying is a new way of replacing meditation to release stress.

10. Whenever your heart starts beating fast you get excited because you're reminded of your favorite disco tune.

The opposite of a Low Density Lifestyle is a High Density Lifestyle. This way of living sooner or later creates blockages, or density, in the body and mind. When there's high density in the body it can measurably be observed as high blood pressure, along with high levels of plaque, cholesterol, triglycerides, low density lipoproteins (whereas a Low Density Lifestyle is the right kind of LDL, low density lipoproteins are the wrong kind of LDL), and other markers of negative blood chemistry. A person with high density in their body and mind will suffer from chronic health problems, and also will be prone to rigid and inflexible thinking.

While achieving a Low Density Lifestyle might at first take some work—work that will pay off in tremendous dividends—a High Density Lifestyle actually at first takes no work at all, because it occurs when you go through your day on autopilot, oblivious to your body, environment and relationships. But once you make the commitment to living a Low Density Lifestyle, the opposite will become true, and your ability to attain a Low Density Lifestyle will become automatic.

As the density, or blockages, in the body build up over time, achieving a Low Density Lifestyle becomes more difficult. But as long as you have a pulse, it is not impossible. It just might take more work.

One of the key factors in determining whether you are living a Low or High Density Lifestyle is the amount of stress and overstimulation in your life. The greater these are, the more the body will produce excess amounts of adrenaline, cortisol and other fat-soluble steroids, in order to keep you in fight-or-flight mode and capable of staving off what is perceived as a threat to your existence.

The problem with these chemicals is that they cause tangible densities in the body to develop. Once they are manufactured, because of their fat-soluble nature, the body doesn't easily metabolize them, leaving their toxic chemical residues to linger in the blood stream and be stored in various regions. The end result is damage to the body, and it can be severe.

Another unfortunate aspect of a High Density Lifestyle is its relationship to dogmatic and inflexible thinking. When you are living a High Density Lifestyle, your thought field becomes heavy and opaque. A thick fog of negativity permeates your body; this cloud contains a knot of tired and draining emotions, including fear, anger, frustration, anxiety, depression and resentment.

These negative thought patterns can become so ingrained in the body that they begin to ingratiate themselves into specific regions, lodging in the muscles, joints, bones, organs and connective tissue. Needless to say, this situation can bring about system overload and breakdown, and can cause chronic and degenerative physical illness.

Part of the problem is that negativity pervades our collective unconscious. It is omnipresent as a force in our lives. It is a dark energy field that easily gets embedded into the mind, body and soul of most people. Even if you are a staunch nonbeliever in energy, it is not hard to relate to the effects of prolonged stress on your body.

Once the negative energy field becomes entrenched in the body it develops properties similar to a lead shield. A lead shield has enough high level density to block radiation and most frequencies and waves. A dense negative energy field in the body is capable of blocking frequencies and wavelengths that circulate throughout the universe. By blocking these signals, it stops the body and mind from receiving communication from the Zero-Point Field, in the process impeding your ability to use your greater potential.

But it doesn't have to be this way. Having high levels of density in the body is not a death sentence. It's just a matter of moving the stagnation in the body, opening the pathways of energy and letting things flow. This isn't rocket science. It may take work, it may be a process, you may have to be patient, but it can be done.

Candace Pert, the former researcher at the National Institutes of Health and author of the landmark book, *Molecules of Emotion*, said:

> My research has shown me that when emotions are expressed—which is to say that the biochemicals that are the substrate of emotion are flowing freely—all systems are united and made whole. When emotions are repressed, denied, not allowed to be whatever they may be, our network pathways get blocked, stopping the flow of the vital feel-good, unifying chemicals that run both our biology and our behavior.

The greatest chemical component of the body is water, and water, no matter how hard you try to dam it, will always seek and find an open pathway to flow. If you open the dam in your body, and allow the blockages to dissolve, you will find the path to true health and happiness—the Low Density Lifestyle.

"Water flows in places men reject and so is like the Tao," Lao Tzu wrote in the *Tao Te Ching*. The wisdom of the sages holds true in any age.

3

How Did We Get Here?

One who asks a question is a fool for five minutes; one who does not ask a question remains a fool forever. – Chinese proverb

The ability to simplify means to eliminate the unnecessary so that the necessary may speak. – Hans Hofmann

The truth is that our finest moments are most likely to occur when we are feeling deeply uncomfortable, unhappy, or unfulfilled. For it is only in such moments, propelled by our discomfort, that we are likely to step out of our ruts and start searching for different ways or truer answers.
– M. Scott Peck

How have we gotten so far off the beaten track that we've forgotten how to slow down and find our calm and peaceful center of balance? In so many ways big and small, it's because we've lost our orientation. We've become such a fast-paced society, accustomed to instant gratification and the achievement of immediate results. We're impatient and have to have it now.

We've lost perspective, the ability to look at the big picture, and the capability to plan for long-term results. We've forgotten when you plant a seed, you have to cultivate the soil and give it time in order for it to sprout and come to life.

Furthermore, we aren't willing to look within, to examine our values and question whether our life has meaning.

We are starved for meaning and searching for something to grasp. But we just keep barreling forward, immune to the signs that something might be missing, until one day when we get hit over the head by something huge, some major life-changing, and at times life-shattering, event that seemingly comes out of nowhere.

We are a society lacking in wisdom, and as such, we are floundering, unable to question whether the path we are on, which is a road filled with many deep-rooted and unsustainable problems, is a dead-end path. It truly is, but the direction we are going is hurtling in the wrong direction.

We cannot take for granted the status quo; we need to ask the hard questions and be willing to dig for the answers, even if they will make us deeply uncomfortable.

If we don't get off of this High Density Lifestyle path, it will lead to catastrophic consequences. By settling for the status quo, and choosing to be comfortable with what isn't working, we have left the hard questions for future generations. And they may not have the luxury of time to answer them.

I've been often asked: what percentage of the population, or at least the American population, do you feel is living a High Density Lifestyle? My answer is that if you asked me that 100 years ago, I would have said 35%; if you had asked me that 50 years ago, I would have said 65%; if you had asked me that 30 years ago, I would have said 75%; if you would have asked me that 10 years ago, I would have said 90%; but now, in the present day, my answer is 98%.

We are a busy, information-rich culture, but something has been lost, and that is our hearts. We are drowning in information but starved for knowledge. We are full of technical know-how but lacking in wisdom and intuition. We have complicated and cluttered our lives, and have forgotten the beauty and value of simplicity. We search for our happiness through external things, forgetting that happiness is created from within.

We are sleepwalking through our days, instead of being fully present, fully aware and fully awake. But it doesn't have to be that way.

Part II: How to Achieve a Low Density Lifestyle:

A 12-Step Guide to Becoming FREE

4

Diet and Nutrition

It's bizarre that the produce manager is more important to my children's health than the pediatrician. - Meryl Streep

He that takes medicine and neglects diet, wastes the skill of the physician. - Chinese Proverb

The wise man should consider that health is the greatest of human blessings. Let food be your medicine. - Hippocrates

It all starts with what we eat. It isn't rocket science to understand that what you put in your mouth has a profound bearing on your health and your ability to live a Low Density Lifestyle. If you eat foods that inflame and clog the gut, arteries, organs and cells, they will create blockages and densities in the body.

The modern day diet is quite toxic to the body and will lead you in the direction of a High Density Lifestyle. And as you cascade down the rocky road of a High Density Lifestyle, your health will become more precarious as chronic illnesses set in. Many times these chronic illnesses are so subtle that they go by unnoticed or are considered just part of "getting old."

Most of the foods of the modern day lifestyle create inflammation inside your body. Inflammation is an important mechanism of the body when it is faced with an acute situation, such as a cut or infection. In that case, the body creates the inflammatory process in order to go into repair mode to heal what is going on.

But if the body has to constantly create the inflammatory process to deal with upsets, such as the introduction of poor quality, toxic and extremely dense foods into the body, after awhile it will become overwhelmed and not be capable of creating the proper response. In that case, the body will stay in an inflammatory state, which is detrimental to the body. Chronic inflammation in the body generates a constant supply of free radicals that overwhelm the body's defenses and will damage the DNA machinery, putting us on the treadmill of chronic and degenerative illness.

The modern diet is rich in compounds that cause inflammatory states, and lacks antioxidants and other nutrients that stop the inflammatory process. These compounds include a number of foods and food categories that are common to today's eating habits. Let's examine them:

1) **Refined carbohydrates**—white flour, white rice, sugar, white bread, white pasta, breakfast cereals, cookies, cakes, candy, soda, chips, pretzels, etc.

2) **Hydrogenated oils**—these are the trans-fatty acids that you find in candy, baked goods, margarine, chips, peanut butter, fast foods and commercially processed vegetable oils.

3) **Processed meats**—foods such as

DIET AND NUTRITION

lunchmeats, hot dogs and sausages are laden with chemicals like nitrates that have been shown to be carcinogenic and will cause inflammation in the body.

4) Saturated fats—will cause inflammation in the body, along with quickly creating blockages and densities. Saturated fats are found in meats, dairy products and eggs. If you choose to eat meats, stick with less dense meats such as fish and lean poultry.

5) In today's High Density Lifestyle, due to the increased toxic load in our body, foods that were typically healthful to our bodies have now become common offenders. The latest research in clinical nutrition has now included nuts, gluten, soy, corn, dairy, and eggs as common allergens for many of us. These foods have been linked to a number of sub-clinical and subtle health problems. Reactions to these foods have been linked to physical, neurological and emotional problems.

All these categories of foods will create inflammation and blockages in the body, thereby decreasing your ability to live a Low Density Lifestyle. Eating these foods will impede your circulation and energy flow, and cause you to feel heavy, lethargic and out of synch with your body. Neither your body nor mind will feel right when you eat a regular diet of these foods because your body will be in a high-density state.

There are many categories of foods that are beneficial for helping you feel healthier, in the flow, lighter and less dense. A diet high in fresh (and preferably organic) grains, vegetables, legumes, fruits, nuts and seeds will do wonders. In addition, there are some categories and foods to include regularly that are strong anti-inflammatory agents. These include:

> 1) **Omega-3 essential fatty acids**—found in certain fish, walnuts, flax and pumpkin seeds. You can also take them in supplement form.
> 2) **Olive oil and other cold processed vegetable oils.**
> 3) **Good quality protein**—Nuts, legumes, seeds, tofu, fish and lean poultry.
> 4) **Dark green leafy vegetables and green and brightly colored vegetables**—these have a strong anti-inflammatory effect on the body.
> 5) **Berries, especially blueberries, strawberries, pomegranate and goji berries, along with brightly colored fruit**—these also have a strong anti-inflammatory effect on the body.
> 6) **Supplementation**—certain supplements can be quite helpful, and these include Vitamin B complex, Vitamins C, D and E, plus CoQ10 and Beta-Carotene.

In addition, it is important that the beverages you drink are not ones that can cause inflammation and blockages in the body. The best thing to drink as your primary beverage is water—pure, clean water. If you are getting water from your tap, make sure it runs through a filter first, so as to clean out the chemicals and heavy metals that are found in most municipal drinking systems. Other good things to drink are vegetable and fruit juices, herbal teas and shakes and smoothies, if they are made from high quality ingredients.

One other category to touch on that are outstanding foods that can help clear out blockages and densities in the body and can aid you in achieving a Low Density Lifestyle are the so-called superfoods.

Three well-known foods in this category are Blue-Green Algae, Chlorella and Spirulina—they are high in mineral and protein content and can bind with heavy metals and carry them out of the body. Foods that have the ability to bind with heavy metals are an integral part of a Low Density Lifestyle (kelp and sea vegetables are another category of superfoods that can do this).

Heavy metals are toxic substances that if ingested, lodge in the body's fatty tissues and can bind with other cellular material to cause very dense blockages. They are commonly found in foods laden with preservatives; meats from farm-raised animals that have been injected with or fed antibiotics or growth hormones; medications; unfiltered water; and even the mercury that is used to fill the cavities in our teeth. If you eat foods that can help remove these heavy metals, such as the above superfoods, you will doing your body a great service and will be well on your way to living a Low Density Lifestyle.

By following the advice in this chapter—cutting out the anti-inflammatory foods and eating a whole foods oriented diet, along with certain supplementation, you will feel much more healthier and more in the flow.

One other thing to point out is that it would also be wise to eat less in general. To be part of a Low Density Lifestyle means to feel light of body and mind, and when you eat a lot, you feel heavy, and when you eat less, your body feels lighter.

Many cultures believe that you should only eat when hungry, and then you should only eat to 80% capacity. Furthermore, they state that a person should not eat for three hours before going to sleep, in order to allow the food to digest. Some cultures even include fasting as a regular part of dietary regimen, so that the digestive tract can rest and the body can clear out the waste matter that builds up on the inside. These traditional concepts are wise things to integrate into a regular dietary practice.

5

Health and Wellness

The first wealth is health. - Ralph Waldo Emerson

Please keep in mind the distinction between healing and treatment: treatment originates from outside, whereas healing comes from within. - Andrew Weil

The doctor of the future will give no medicine, but will interest his patients in the care of the human frame, and in the cause and prevention of disease. - Thomas Edison

Eating well is the foundation for feeling better, but the cultivation of overall good health and wellness is ultimately about developing the right approach and mindset. If you do that, good health becomes easy to achieve and maintain.

Being in good health allows you to easily live a Low Density Lifestyle, while being in ill health is not conducive to it. Unfortunately, most people are walking around in poor health, and are taking medications in order that they can function, be productive and carry on in their daily routine.

Medications have a number of inherent problems, and do not help to restore health. All they do at best is arrest symptoms and keep you functioning. They can cause side effects that range from mild to severe, can be toxic to the liver and kidneys, can depress the immune system and can lead to other long-term health problems.

The key to developing good health is empowering yourself to be proactive. If you are not feeling well, this is a signal from the body that something is amiss. If you learn to listen to what the body is saying, and take that message to heart, you will be able to start becoming healthier.

One of the inevitable side effects of a High Density Lifestyle is illness. Just the stress of living this way will sooner or later catch up to you. But if you start listening to your body, you will start to understand when the body is telling you that you are overtaxed. Instead of rushing to take a drug for the symptoms you are experiencing from living a High Density Lifestyle, if you learn to slow down, that by itself will do you wonders.

Now, I'm not saying that you should never take a medication—there are times when they are necessary, but they should only be seen as a bridge, a temporary remedy while you work on the permanent solution.

The great majority of people seek out a doctor when they are not feeling well, with the hope that the doctor will have the answers. But did you know that most physicians are immersed in a High Density Lifestyle? A study published in the September 2008 *Annals of Internal Medicine* found that when physicians are in medical school, 50% suffer from burnout and 10% consider suicide. If this is what they go through when they are trained, how can the profession be of help in understanding how to help a person get off the treadmill of a High Density Lifestyle?

Seeking out a permanent solution may require you to see a health provider, but this health provider may not be a physician. They may be an acupuncturist, naturopath, homeopath, herbalist, chiropractor, body worker, energy worker, therapist, or a practitioner of some other treatment modality. Or you may see a few practitioners, including a physician, to meet your needs. Whoever you see, it's best if you envisioned them as part of a team, and that you, as the person who knows you the best, as the director of the team.

Often, the body seems to work in mysterious ways that seem confounding for someone not trained in medicine and health. But the body is not that complicated; you can train yourself to think in the same way that outstanding health providers think and learn to figure out what is going on when you are not feeling well.

The good health providers think like detectives and try to decipher what is going on in the body by trying to understand what it is that the body is attempting to communicate. The detective work will investigate diet and lifestyle and see if these factors are playing a primary role in causing illness.

By carefully going over the diet and by looking at the various aspects of someone's life—their work, relationships, stresses, attitude, passions and other things—the answer is usually found.

If you are willing to take the time to honestly look at your life and assess it, you can figure it out on your own, although often times an objective person is required to help you to understand your life and get you standing back on your own two feet.

If you are willing to go this route, you will become healthier and in the Low Density Lifestyle. Once you are in this mode, your health approach will change to one oriented towards wellness and prevention, and when you see a health provider, that person will most probably be a practitioner of holistic medicine, and your visits will be wellness oriented.

For instance, in ancient China, people traditionally saw an acupuncturist once every season, for their seasonal "tune-up." This helped keep them healthy through the season. Ironically in our society, we take our car in for a seasonal tune-up so that the car can run well for the duration of the season, while neglecting to do anything proactive for ourselves.

If you take care of your health by taking a proactive stance, it will pay itself off in huge dividends. You will feel physically and mentally better, and be capable of living more in the flow. An Arabic proverb says it well: "He who has health has hope; and he who has hope has everything."

6

Movement and Exercise

Everything is in motion. Everything flows. Everything is vibrating.
- Wayne Dyer

Breath, movement, intent, hesitation, stillness as a posture are all manifesting both the flow of the movement and the result of that flow.
- Cherie Hanson

Dance is the hidden language of the soul. - Martha Graham

We were born to move. Movement is essential to life—it helps get the circulation of blood and energy in your body flowing better. Too much of a sedentary lifestyle is not conducive to living a Low Density Lifestyle.

Movement of and by itself, no matter what type, by virtue of its ability to get the heart pumping and blood flowing, can help take lactic acid and other toxic waste matter that build up in the muscles, organs and connective tissue and assist the body in metabolizing and excreting them. This can help to dissipate the blockages and densities in the body.

At the same time, there is an art to movement. Even though we are always in motion, and always doing things, there is a certain approach to movement that can greatly enhance being in the flow state. When you approach movement from this way, you will be practicing effortless effort and become more attuned to your body. It will heighten your awareness, still your mind and allow you to activate more of your potential—and by doing so, allow you to become more FREE.

The type of movement I am talking about is any type of movement that touches your soul—what your passion is may be different from someone else's. But the key is to do something that is aimed at the mind-body unison. What would be best is if the approach focused on a number of things: the body, the mind, the energy system, the breath and stillness.

Granted, there may not be one approach you're doing that might fit the bill and meet all these needs. But that's ok. The trend nowadays is cross-training, to do a number of things that touch on each of the key areas that need attention.

The best philosophy in determining what type of movement to engage in, in order to overcome blockages and density in the body, and allow you to attain a Low Density Lifestyle, is to practice an approach or approaches that both elongate your muscles and strengthen them. You need both—one creates flexibility and the other strength, and they go hand in hand in helping to create a dynamic flow in the body and mind.

There are many approaches that aim for this: from the East we have Tai Chi, Aikido, Kung Fu and other martial arts, along with Yoga; from the West we have Pilates, resistance work using a ball or bands, and strength training. Then, of course, there are the various sports, which can put you profoundly in the zone when you become deeply immersed in them; and there is also dance, a modality that has its origins in the primal rhythms of the universe.

Some people will mistakenly think that living a Low Density Lifestyle means having a body without muscle tone; they picture the image of a blissed-out wandering mendicant who has not a care in the world. That is because many spiritual traditions caution followers to turn away from the body because they believe it to be a trap set by the ego to hinder transcendence.

But this is far from the truth. Whether you're seeking spiritual harmony, soulful pleasures, or just want to sweat, training the body is as important as training the mind and spirit—you can't have one without the other, and they are deeply interconnected. That is not to say that you have to have abs of steel to attain the Low Density Lifestyle; instead what is important is an approach to movement that focuses on flexibility and strength, and touches on the components that help to make us FREE: the body, the mind, the energy system, the breath and stillness.

You may wonder why stillness is mentioned when it is movement I am talking about. Stillness gives the body a chance to rest and regenerate, and for the internal computer that runs our body and mind to reset the hardware and software within us. You can't just push, push, push all the time—we do too much of that. Taking the time to be still and to relax helps the body get into the effortless effort mode, and when we are in that mode we are more capable of feeling the pulse of the universe vibrating deep within our soul.

We also can't ignore the importance of the breath, and when we practice stillness we become more cognizant of the breath and our breathing patterns. Breath is essential to all the processes that occur in the body; in Eastern traditions breath is essential because it is known that being in tune with your breath connects you to your deepest inner knowing.

The breath also signals both the beginning and end of life. If you have ever been present at the passing of a life, you would have witnessed that the final sign of transition is a deep and freeing gasp. In contrast, if you have ever had the pleasure of being witness to a new life about to begin its journey, you would have seen that the first sign of life is the cry of a newborn baby as they claim their place in the world.

Author Tarthand Tulku in his book *Tibetan Meditation* notes that we have both an outer and inner breath: the outer breath is our physical respiration, while the inner breath silently moves through the body and is smooth and full of feeling, and as it circulates throughout, has powerful effects on our energy centers.

If all you ever do is push, push, push all the time with your movement approach, and for that matter in your everyday doings, and never practice stillness and awareness of breath, your body will just become tighter and more rigid. That is not the way to be if you want to live up to your peak abilities and enjoy the bounty of life. There is a certain lightness of spirit and soul that is desired in order to live a more zestful life, and so your movement philosophy should make sure that is what is represented in your approach.

That's not to say that at times you won't sweat and strain and feel sore all over, but you should also make the time to do something kinesthetic that has a different orientation: one that encompasses stillness, quiet and awareness of breath, so that you can feed and nourish the soul.

There also are many times when your movements are just natural extensions of life. Gardening, walking, hiking, biking, baking, playing with your friends or kids, and many other things that are part of the everyday aspects of life are all important ingredients to a healthy life because they are part of the ebb and flow of the cycles of nature and the changing seasons.

Thomas Jefferson understood this very thing when he once said, "walking is the best possible exercise. Habituate yourself to walk very far." And the Zen proverb "chop wood, carry water" is a reminder that in the daily routines of life, we can find harmony, increased awareness, stillness and flexibility of body and mind, all of which will help point you towards a Low Density Lifestyle.

7

Flexibility of Mind and Body

Nothing in the world is more flexible and yielding than water. Yet when it attacks the firm and the strong, none can withstand it, because they have no way to change it. So the flexible overcome the adamant, the yielding overcome the forceful. Everyone knows this, but no one can do it. – Lao Tzu

I am a man of fixed and unbending principles, the first of which is to be flexible at all times. – Everett Dirksen

In the future, instead of striving to be right at a high cost, it will be more appropriate to be flexible and plural at a lower cost. If you cannot accurately predict the future then you must flexibly be prepared to deal with various possible futures. – Edward de Bono

In the previous chapter I discussed movement as a means to accentuate the flow state. By moving is such a way, it will help you to become more fluid and flexible of body.

I would say that even more important than being flexible of body is being flexible of mind. Without the ability to be fluid and flexible in your thought process, you will have a hard time navigating life. That is because change is the one constant of life, and in order to steer through the winds of change, you have to be flexible and adaptable.

The art of living lies in constant readjustment to your surroundings. The worst thing you can be is unyielding, unbending and dogmatic in your thinking. There is always something that will come around the bend that will challenge you to think different and cause you to have to rearrange your preconceived notions.

Think of yourself as a scientist, even if you miserably failed every high school science class you took. In its purest form, science is the search for truth, no matter the consequences, no matter what sacred cows might be upended. Of course, in modern science the opposite is true—the level of rigid and inflexible thinking in science and medicine is astounding, and no matter how much a fact may overturn a theory, the theory will stay put if it is too upsetting to have to get rid of it. In fact, there is a saying that the great tragedy of science is the slaying of a beautiful hypothesis by an ugly fact.

Our universe is an open-ended one, and the more open we stay to possibilities, the more resonant we are to the permutations of life. Even the global economy is working its way to becoming more of an open-source one, where people can add layers and textures to work others have done before, without the concern of trespassing. In the digital age, claims of ownership are being re-thought, as the desire now is to make things more accessible and easier to be shared. This is the by-product of an economy where things are becoming more open and flexible.

Yet most people are still fighting, still not willing to accept change. They would rather fight than switch, preferring to be closed and inflexible rather than being open and flexible. It's so much easier to be flexible than inflexible; it's so jarring on the body and mind to hold firm to something when it's obvious it's wrong.

FLEXIBILITY OF MIND AND BODY

The former Monty Python star John Cleese said:

> We all operate in two contrasting modes, which might be called open and closed. The open mode is more relaxed, more receptive, more exploratory, more democratic, more playful and more humorous. The closed mode is the tighter, more rigid, more hierarchical, more tunnel-visioned. Most people unfortunately spend most of their time in the closed mode. Not that the closed mode cannot be helpful. If you are leaping a ravine, the moment of takeoff is a bad time for considering alternative strategies. When you charge the enemy machine-gun post, don't waste energy trying to see the funny side of it. Do it in the "closed" mode. But the moment the action is over, try to return to the "open" mode—to open your mind again to all the feedback from our action that enables us to tell whether the action has been successful, or whether further action is needed to improve on what we have done. In other words, we must return to the open mode, because in that mode we are the most aware, most receptive, most creative, and therefore at our most intelligent.

What John Cleese says is so true. When you are flexible and fluid of body and mind, you are operating at full capacity, and you can start living to your fullest potential. Everything is then flowing and you are going at it on all cylinders.

As any jazz musician knows, it takes flexibility and adaptability for improvisation to create beauty. Jazz musicians are well trained in standard theory and principles of music, but by virtue of their willingness to discard certain conventions they are able to create new rules, which then leads them to new forms and sounds.

8

Mindfulness

Life is now. There was never a time when your life was not now, nor will there ever be.
- Eckhart Tolle

You can observe a lot by watching. - Yogi Berra

The moment one gives close attention to anything, even a blade of grass, it becomes a mysterious, awesome, indescribably magnificent world in itself. - Henry Miller

Mindfulness is the art of being aware, and fully present, in the moment. When practicing mindfulness, you become aware of your thoughts, your actions and your movements. Although mindfulness stems from the Buddhist tradition, it is not an approach that is native to Buddhism or any other religion or philosophy.

Mindfulness involves becoming aware of the mind's chattering, and observing the continual commentary that is going on. By doing this you can discern if the thoughts have value, or if they are just the same old same old—meaning whether they are observations based on deeper truths, or whether they are negative thought patterns that rule your life.

If you become more mindful and more aware of your thoughts and actions, you will be able to understand why you are acting the way you are, and whether your reactions are knee-jerk and reflexive. This is a key step to living a Low Density Lifestyle, because once you become more aware of negative reactions, you can begin to let them go. And by letting them go, the blockages and densities in the body and mind that are aided and abetted by these negative thought patterns can start to dissipate, allowing you to become FREE.

Mindfulness also leads to a more awakened life, a life that feels more alive and grounded. Some people say that as they became more mindful they feel like they no longer sleepwalk through existence.

Mindfulness leads to a finely tuned sense of alertness, a sharpened and heightened clarity of the five senses, and the ability to achieve an unbiased and highly objective perspective of life, grounded in direct experiencing alone.

According to Buddhism the four foundations of mindfulness are: contemplation of the body; contemplation of feelings; contemplation of the mind; and contemplation of mental objects.

These four foundations can be explored through a formal meditation practice, or informally by completely paying attention throughout the routines of everyday life. If practiced formally as a meditation, it is achieved by concentrating on the mind as you sit in quiet contemplation. As you meditate, you witness your thoughts, feelings, bodily sensations and state of mind. You observe them and notice if they have value or if they are just idle chatter. If they are thoughts that have no bearing on reality or truth, you release them and let them go.

If mindfulness is practiced informally by being present in the moment throughout the day, then the key is to become fully aware of your actions and reactions in all situations. For instance, if you were in a situation that makes you angry, then you would witness your anger and explore what it is about the situation that makes you angry. You may discover that the anger is a byproduct of the way you see the world, and your way of seeing the world may be checkered by your negative thought patterns. You can then explore this further to understand what these thought patterns are, and how they hold you back and lock you into a High Density Lifestyle.

Whether mindfulness is practiced formally or informally, it can help you understand your negative thought patterns and your fears, and the habits that these fears produce. We cannot become free of our habits unless first we identify them by bringing them to the surface.

I often suggest to people, as a way to help get them started on the path to mindfulness, to take one thing that they do on an everyday basis and do it mindfully. It could be brushing your teeth, combing your hair, eating breakfast, or any of the myriad things that are done everyday—and are usually done on automatic pilot.

If you do just one thing a day mindfully, you are way ahead of the curve. From there you can then graduate to doing two mindful things a day. And as you master that, you can continue on and make most of your daily life a mindful one. Like any learned trait, the more it gets practiced, the more it becomes second nature.

Another exercise to help hone your mindfulness skills is to get together with another person and sit and face one another. One person can talk for a few minutes as the other person listens while looking into the eyes of the speaker. The person speaking can speak of matters profound or mundane, it isn't important. What is important is that the person listening fully listens and doesn't interrupt the speaker.

After a few minutes, roles can be switched and the person who listened can now be the speaker, and the person who was the speaker can now be the listener. Again, as the speaker talks, the other person will listen with all their attention.

Once you are done with the exercise, take turns talking about it and how it felt to be listened to, and to have listened.

Usually when people have a conversation, listening is done on a half-hearted basis. The person listening often is drifting off and thinking of other things, or is gearing up to interrupt the speaker by saying something, whether related to the conversation or not.

As you become more mindful, you pay better attention to everything around you. Due to a heightened sense of clarity, you become more acutely aware of your surroundings and environment.

This is why the Buddha said, "If we could see the miracle of a single flower clearly, our whole life would change." As was said earlier in this chapter, mindfulness leads to a finely tuned sense of alertness and a sharpened and heightened clarity of the five senses. It can allow us, as the poet William Blake wrote, in "Auguries of Innocence":

> To see a World in a grain of sand
> And a Heaven in a Wild Flower,
> Hold Infinity in the Palm of your hand
> And Eternity in an Hour.

Leonardo da Vinci is widely considered a universal genius, and is also a prime example of both a master of mindfulness and of having lived a Low Density Lifestyle. His genius was predicated on his ability to give single-minded focus and attention to his surroundings and environment, and it was this that allowed his creativity to flower. He found that his focus permitted him to become fully aware and fully mindful, and to be able to use all his senses. Da Vinci said that his powers of observation were an important key to his ability to think creatively.

Da Vinci was gifted with exceptional powers of observation and used those powers ingeniously. By applying mindfulness to his daily life, and being astute in his observations of the natural world and the human world, he was able to live a Low Density Lifestyle and tap into the Zero-Point Field and the creative powers of the universe.

Mindfulness is an essential ingredient to living a Low Density Lifestyle. By being present and in the moment, you are able to fully observe your thoughts, your actions and your reactions, and you can more fully understand how all your negative thought patterns—which create the preconceptions and dogmas that you live by—stop you from becoming FREE.

Take a walk down your street, or in nature, and closely observe everything around you. Stop, look, smell, touch, feel and listen. Make every step you take one in which you are fully present in your body. You will be astounded by what you truly see, and you will realize how much you have missed by not being mindful.

The key is to be fully in your body, and aware of every step you take. The opposite of that is to be like Mr. James Duffy, one of the characters from James Joyce's *Dubliners*, who, as Joyce wrote, "lived at a little distance from his body."

A writer who has made a career of his mindful observations of human nature and the natural world is the American author William Least Heat-Moon. In a trilogy of best-selling books, *Blue Highways*, *PrairyErth* and *River Horse*, he writes about his travels and the people, customs and geography he comes across along the way.

Blue Highway is a chronicle of Least Heat-Moon's three-month-long road trip across America, driving along only secondary roads and avoiding cities, making his way into towns like Nameless, Tennessee; Grayville, Illinois; and Bagley, Minnesota. Along the way, he discovers segments of the country that fly under the radar, and Least Heat-Moon perceptively comments on the people he meets and their lives.

In *PrairyErth*, the author takes the reader on a journey through one American county, Chase County, Kansas, one of the last remaining regions of the tallgrass prairies and grasslands that used to cover much of the American Midwest. Least Heat-Moon conducts this journey primarily on foot, and his meticulous observations of people, nature, fence posts and arrowheads create an evocative feel for the land and rural lifestyle in the sparsely populated county.

In *River Horse*, the final volume of his trilogy, Least Heat-Moon writes of his four-month 5,000-mile coast-to-coast boat trip across the U.S., using only the nation's waterways. His stories, chronicles and details of the people he meets, the dangerous weather and floods, the landscapes untouched by time, and the generosity of strangers is, as was his other two books, masterful expositions. His mindful and keen insights into the hearts and minds of the people he comes in contact with lend credence to the notion that most people are good and decent by nature and carry in their hearts incredible resources of inner strength.

These traits are innate in each of us, and can flourish with enough nourishment and cultivation. These also are the traits of a person who lives a Low Density Lifestyle.

The reason William Least Heat-Moon's books are optimistic by nature is because the more mindful and acutely aware you become of your surroundings, as Least Heat-Moon did, and the more you observe the human condition, the more you comprehend that most people are by nature good, and are searching for happiness, joy, hope and love for themselves and to share with others.

When you practice mindfulness and come across a jaded, pessimistic and stressed-out soul, your keen observations can allow you to become aware of what is eating at their psyche. Everyone, even the least happiest amongst us, can be touched by words that are truthful, authentic, loving and have vision as their guiding force. By mindfully understanding this person's angst, you can offer the kind of help that can soothe their savage soul and help guide them towards a Low Density Lifestyle.

9

Integrity

*Live in such a way that you would not be
ashamed to sell your parrot to the town gossip.
- Will Rogers*

*Better keep yourself clean and bright; you are the window through
which you must see the world. - George Bernard Shaw*

*You can out-distance that which is running after you,
but not what is running inside you.
- Rwandan Proverb*

Integrity is, according to the dictionary definition, "The quality of possessing and steadfastly adhering to high moral principles or professional standards." It is when what we say is the same as what we do—we live by our word and are true to ourselves.

Ralph Waldo Emerson said, "Nothing is at last sacred but the integrity of your own mind." If you live by your word you will live in pretty elite company, because not everyone is willing to sign onto that covenant.

It seems so simple—live with integrity and tell the truth, because then you have nothing to hide or fear. When you don't tell the truth, when you continually lie to others and yourself, the deceits start building up in your body to the point that you become twisted in knots. As it happens more and more, and the knots get thicker and thicker, the deceits turn into densities that begin to calcify in your body, creating imbalances of body and mind. In this case you are living by the credo of Sir Walter Scott's famous couplet: "Oh, what a tangled web we weave / When first we practice to deceive!"

You know how you feel when you tell the truth—you can feel the smooth flow of energy coursing through your body. You feel light of spirit, relaxed and bright.

Contrast that with when you don't tell the truth. When you don't, your muscles tighten and you become defensive and guarded, like an animal backed up against the wall. Your spirit negatively transforms and becomes heavy and dense.

Abraham Lincoln said, "When I do good, I feel good. When I do bad, I feel bad. That's my religion." It's that simple. When you do good, you feel good because the body goes into a flow state, and when you do bad, you feel bad because your body tightens up and becomes more dense.

Just as Abraham Lincoln said, it is like a religion. When you operate with integrity, and feel lighter of spirit, you resonate with the Zero-Point Field, the focal point of the universe that is the origin of life and continually teems with infinite energy and information. When you are in that state, it is akin to a religious experience, because you are one with the pulse of the universe and living a Low Density Lifestyle.

When you lack integrity, as your body tightens up from the tangled web you weave (created from the web of lies you spin), an energetic field that is akin to a dense lead shield positions itself outside your body and blocks you from picking up the frequencies and wavelengths that emanate from the Zero-Point Field. This cuts you off from the pulse of the universe; instead you become a prisoner in a cell of your own making, living amidst the High Density Lifestyle.

"Integrity is the essence of everything successful," the visionary architect, inventor and philosopher Buckminster Fuller said. And Warren Buffett, the Oracle of Omaha, once said, "In looking for people to hire, you look for three qualities: integrity, intelligence, and energy. And if they don't have the first, the other two will kill you."

They are both so very right. As I said, integrity gives you a direct pipeline to the Zero-Point Field, and when you tap into the universal field you feel your most vital and alive, and you are capable of using much more of your potential.

When you operate without integrity, you look out only for your own self-interests. When that happens, it's easy to be overcome by greed and unprincipled behavior. And as you continue to act in this way you will hurt and betray many because you won't care what you say or do, as long as it gets you where you want to go. Your mantra becomes "the ends justify the means."

Niccolo Machiavelli devised the expression, "The ends justify the means," when he wrote it in his notorious treatise, *The Prince*, in 1513. Written as a guide to gaining and holding power, his name has become synonymous with ruthless politics, deceit and the pursuit of power by any means.

But living a life in this manner catches up to you sooner or later. You may experience short-term gain, but at a very large price—selling your soul.

By living a life of integrity you may not achieve success as quickly as by living a life of deceit, but the ride getting to your successful destination will be an enjoyable one, because your journey will take place along the path of the Low Density Lifestyle. And when you finally get to your endpoint, it will truly feel like manna from heaven, because you can say that you did it your way, the way of integrity.

10

Attitude and Emotions

The greatest discovery of my generation is that human beings can alter their lives by altering their attitudes of mind. - William James

The state of your life is nothing more than a reflection of your state of mind.
- Wayne Dyer

The basic thing is that everyone wants happiness, no one wants suffering. And happiness mainly comes from our own attitude, rather than from external factors. If your own mental attitude is correct, even if you remain in a hostile atmosphere, you feel happy.
- The Dalai Lama

Our mindset and way of seeing the world play a big role in how we carry ourselves through life. If we see the world as a harsh and difficult place, then things will always seem harsh and difficult. And if we see the world as a wondrous place, full of challenges and surprises, then things will present themselves in that way.

The secret to happiness and living a Low Density Lifestyle is truly in our attitude and emotions. If you hold onto negative and unresolved emotions, such as anger, resentment, fear, shame and jealousy, it will weigh you down, and cause your body and mind to feel heavy and dense. This will permeate into your attitude and become your raison d'etre, or reason for living. Everything will be seen through the lens of these negative and unresolved emotions.

The energy we put out is the energy we attract, so if you walk around with an attitude formed by a multitude of negative emotions, this is what you attract in your own life.

This is why a High Density Lifestyle feeds on itself and becomes self-perpetuating. If your mindset is one that sees the world through a negative filter, and you attract the very same back, you create a negative feedback loop in which the same negative energy continues to circulate around and around in your life, ad infinitum.

It sounds simple: if you want to change your life, live a Low Density Lifestyle, and be more FREE, all you have to do is change your attitude and be more positive, loving, hopeful and happy.

Yes, this is true, and on the one hand it is simple, yet on the other hand it is not so simple. It may take some work, because many of us have a shadow side, a deeply rooted dark side that silently prefers to sabotage our work. This is another byproduct of a High Density Lifestyle—having densities and blockages in the body that are caused from unresolved emotions that have never worked themselves out and have been left to percolate and fester internally.

You can consider the shadow side to be an arthrosclerosis of the soul. Just as plaque—which is a physical and tangible density—can build up in the arteries and lead to coronary artery disease, so too can unresolved emotions—which we can consider an energetic plaque and an intangible density. This type of plaque clogs the soul and creates an energetic holding pattern in the body and mind that blocks us from achieving the goal of living a Low Density Lifestyle, no matter how much we desire to live that way.

The shadow work you do should be integrated with forgiveness and surrender—both of these are important concepts and are closely entwined. Some of the unresolved emotions may not fully be resolved to your satisfaction, because of a number of reasons: they may deal with someone who passed away; they may pertain to someone you are no longer in contact with; or they just might be difficult situations that allow for no full and transparent resolution. In these cases the best path to resolution is to make peace and let go—to surrender and forgive. Martin Luther King, Jr. once said:

> We must develop and maintain the capacity to forgive. He who is devoid of the power to forgive is devoid of the power to love. There is some good in the worst of us and some evil in the best of us. When we discover this, we are less prone to hate our enemies.

With work you can rid yourself of the energetic holding patterns in your body and mind and transform your life into one that allows you to live the life you were meant to live, one of a Low Density Lifestyle.

Once you get yourself on the right path, it becomes second nature, although you may always have to be vigilant to make sure you maintain the right attitude. Because we live in a world where the vast majority of people have so many unresolved emotions, it's easy to be swayed by the words, actions or energy of others. This is why you have to be attentive and constantly mindful of your thoughts and emotions.

It is like exercising your body—when you do it regularly, the muscles become more flexible and trained to function in a certain way; and when you don't exercise regularly, the muscles begin to atrophy and fall into disuse. So it is with your mind and attitude. By continually exercising them, and always being aware of how you are carrying yourself, you can train your mind to have the right attitude, and to maintain that attitude at all times, no matter what challenges come your way.

This can be called emotional intelligence, which is the ability to be cognizant of your emotions and the way you relate to others. Emotional intelligence, or EQ, has been found to be a greater predictor for success in life than IQ, which had been considered the benchmark for predicting someone's success.

It had been thought that the higher a person's IQ was, the greater they would do in life, because of their high degree of analytic knowledge. But now it is known that what really matters, and what will take you far in life, is whether you have a handle on your emotions and attitude. If you are authentic, and also someone who is positive, calm and collected, and you sincerely care about others, people will respect you, and want to be around you and listen to you, regardless of what your IQ is.

Being emotionally intelligent allows you to have a positive attitude, which allows you to become FREE. To cultivate emotional intelligence may take doing shadow work to help dislodge some of the unresolved emotions within, while at the same time, practicing emotional intelligence (which is closely related to mindfulness), can help keep you maintaining clarity and focus, and to not become a slave to your attitude and emotions.

Daniel Goleman, the author of the landmark book, *Emotional Intelligence*, said:

> Being able to enter flow is emotional intelligence at its best; flow represents perhaps the ultimate in harnessing the emotions in the service of performance and learning. In flow the emotions are not just contained and channeled, but positive, energized, and aligned with the task at hand.

The more emotionally intelligent you are, along with being in the flow and FREE, the healthier are your attitude and emotions. This will only enhance your ability to live a Low Density Lifestyle.

11

Abundance

For true love is inexhaustible; the more you give, the more you have. And if you go to draw at the true fountainhead, the more water you draw, the more abundant is its flow.
– Antoine de Saint-Exupery

The secret of attraction is to love yourself. Attractive people judge neither themselves nor others. They are open to gestures of love. They think about love, and express their love in every action. They know that love is not a mere sentiment, but the ultimate truth at the heart of the universe. – Deepak Chopra

People with a scarcity mentality tend to see everything in terms of win-lose. There is only so much; and if someone else has it, that means there will be less for me. The more principle-centered we become, the more we develop an abundance mentality, the more we are genuinely happy for the successes, well-being, achievements, recognition, and good fortune of other people. We believe their success adds to...rather than detracts from...our lives.
– Stephen R. Covey

If you have an abundance mindset, you understand and recognize that the universe has enough for everyone, and there's enough to go around. Unfortunately, most people live with a mentality of scarcity, and instead see a universe in which there is not enough. If you have that perception, you feel you have to horde things for yourself in order to make sure you get your share before someone comes and takes it from you. A scarcity mindset causes a person to be ruled by greed, self-interest, and self-centeredness.

By living with an attitude of abundance, you have made the decision that you are willing to share of yourself. You intuitively understand that this is a universe that circulates a constant fountain of endlessly flowing energy, and that principle permeates every action you take and every thought you incur.

This type of thinking and action—living in an abundance mindset—is another integral part of being in a flow state and living a Low Density Lifestyle. If you live this way, you embody the notion of a universe as a flowing fountain so intently that you literally and figuratively become the fountain.

To live this way you must be unselfish and carry love for others in your heart. The more you open your heart, the more the abundance flows; the opposite is also true: the less you open your heart, and more closed your heart is, the less abundance flows, and instead the more will you suffer, because you will become small-minded, petty and vindictive, and you will have forgotten the meaning of the Golden Rule: that if you show love to others, they will show love back to you.

There is also the law of karma that gets invoked here, the realization that what goes around, comes around. In other words, if your actions are motivated by the baser self-interests such as greed, then sooner or later it will come back to bite you on your butt.

If you perceive a world in which there is not enough, you become very territorial. You then make sure you get yours before others take it. It becomes a world of us vs. them, a world in which only the fittest survive. Everyday is war and you always have to be ready to do combat in order to keep your fair share. Sounds familiar? This is the way of a High Density Lifestyle.

12

Laughter

The human race has only one really effective weapon and that is laughter. - Mark Twain

What soap is to the body, laughter is to the soul. - Yiddish proverb

There is little success where there is little laughter. - Andrew Carnegie

One of the best ways to feel lighter of body, mind and spirit and to have more health, happiness and joy in your life is to infuse your life with humor and laughter. There's something special about laughter. It allows you to take yourself less seriously, and in the process causes you to lighten up. Comedy, humor and laughter have always been king. They have been an essential part of living since the dawn of humanity.

Instinctively, people have always known that humor and laughter makes you feel better, and because of that, people have been trying to make each other laugh as long as there have been people walking the planet.

It's well known that laughter is good for the health. In one of the most famous and well-documented cases of how laughter can be healing, Norman Cousins, who went on to write about his case in his best-selling book, *Anatomy of an Illness*, healed from a terminal illness by watching funny movies.

The Greek philosopher Aristotle viewed laughter as "a bodily exercise precious to health."

Studies have shown that laughter drops the blood pressure and is linked to healthy function of blood. Laughter appears to cause the tissue that forms the inner lining of blood vessels, the endothelium, to dilate or expand in order to increase blood flow. That makes sense, because when you laugh you can feel your body open up—this is the blood moving through the body and dilating blood vessels.

Other studies have shown that laughter can cause a drop in the blood's concentration of the stress hormone cortisol. Because chronically elevated cortisol levels have been shown to weaken the immune system, this can help ward off disease.

And other experiments have indicated that laughter increases the activity of immune cells called natural killer cells in the saliva of healthy subjects.

Psychologists and mental health experts have also found that laughter and comedy can be a remedy for stress, depression, or just feeling down.

Laughter can also help with pain. As early as 1928, New York physician James J. Walsh noticed that laughter seemed to dampen pain after surgery. Since then, research has indicated that humor can have painkilling properties. One 1996 study demonstrated that patients who watched funny movies needed less of their mild painkillers after orthopedic surgery than did patients who viewed serious flicks or nothing at all.

In addition to suppressing pain, being funny and cheerful can cultivate friendships. Cheerful people have a lighthearted interaction style that facilitates bonding closely with others and builds social support.

And get this, single people: people with a sense of humor may get more dates. In 2006 psychologists Eric R. Bressler of Westfield State College and Sigal Balshine of McMaster University in Ontario reported that women are more likely to consider a man in a photograph a desirable relationship partner if the picture is accompanied by a funny quote attributed to the man. In fact, the women preferred the funny men despite rating them, on average, less intelligent and less trustworthy.

And other research indicates that both men and women value a "sense of humor" when choosing a partner.

According to 18th-century philosopher Immanuel Kant, laughter is one of a trio of tactics humans may use to counterbalance life's troubles. The others are hope and sleep.

So, if you want to lighten up, if you want to live a Low Density Lifestyle, and if you want to get out of the rut of living a High Density Lifestyle, then make sure you have laughter and humor in your life.

Take it from a source no less knowledgeable than Woody Allen, who says, "I am thankful for laughter, except when milk comes out of my nose."

13

The Dreamer

You unlock the door with the key of imagination. - Rod Serling

Nothing happens unless first we dream. - Carl Sandburg

Dream no small dreams for they have no power to move the hearts of men. - Johann Wolfgang Von Goethe

*L*ife is but a dream. Who said that? Was it a famous philosopher, such as Aristotle, Rene Descartes, William James, or Jean-Paul Sartre? Or a famous writer, such as William Shakespeare, Charles Dickens, Kurt Vonnegut or J. K. Rowling?

No, it comes from the English nursery rhyme and song, *Row, Row, Row Your Boat*, written in 1881 by Eliphalet Oram Lyte. Life is but a dream, the last line of the first verse tells us; it is a credo we all would do well to live by.

I'm not saying you should walk around in a perpetual dream state. What I am saying is that being a dreamer—a daydreamer—and using the imagination are an integral part of a Low Density Lifestyle. When we use our capacity to dream and imagine, we are accessing the Zero-Point Field, the Quantum Vacuum, the place of infinite energy and information, and the creative source for the entire universe.

I talked about this in an earlier chapter; about how, if your body and mind are embedded with blockages and densities, you will have a hard time picking up signals from the Zero-Point Field. Yet, if you allow yourself to dream and do it on a constant basis, those signals will eventually make their way to you, because sooner or later the resistance from the densities will let down its guard, allowing some of the signals to filter through.

When you dream and use your imagination, you are tapping into the place where consciousness, stillness, breath and wisdom originate from, the place that Eastern philosophies call Universal Mind, or Big Mind. This might sound mystical, but you have to remember that the source for most famous ideas throughout history have come to their originator in a flash, often when they were least expecting something. The inventor Nicola Tesla said, "Creative ideas come to us like a bolt of lightning."

If you interject a certain amount of dreaminess into your thinking, whether it be daydreaming, gazing into space or applying your night dreams to situations that arise during the day, not only will you begin to think more creatively, you will find your way to a Low Density Lifestyle. And as you find your way there, you will have unlocked the door to the secret of living a life of greater potential.

Albert Einstein, one of the greatest scientists to have graced the earth, understood the importance of dreaming and the imagination. He once said, "Imagination is more important than knowledge. Knowledge is limited; imagination encircles the world."

Whenever you do something creative, be it writing, drawing, playing music, dancing, sculpting, thinking outside the box, or countless other activities, you are entering the flow state by virtue of being able to tap into the creative power of the universe. This is what occurs when you feel your creative juices flowing—you have entered the zone and things become timeless and effortless.

Even some corporations have learned to cultivate the imagination among employees—they understand that workers are more capable of coming up with new ideas when they are given the chance to relax and practice a Low Density Lifestyle. One executive with Nissan Motors said that when his design team gets bogged down, he would find something for the team to do that can take their mind off their work and give them a chance to relax. One thing he does is take the group to the movies. He has found that from doing this, "The tension begins to dissipate. Within days ideas start flowing, knotty problem areas unravel, and the design begins to lead the designers, a sure sign that a strong concept was emerging."

A business consultant, Marsha Madigan, instructs companies that it is the responsibility of leadership to help others use their dreaming abilities and their imagination:

> When leaders see the value of allowing space in between their thoughts, perspective in their thinking, they can see beyond the circumstances and content of problems and situations, to graceful responses and effortless solutions…If we want to change our experience, we need to let go of our current thinking in order to see something new. We need a stance of curiosity, of willingness to give up being 'right,' in order to see what we don't yet

know, in order for a new reality to manifest through us.

Unfortunately, imagination and the dreaming parts of our mind are underutilized. We tend to stay away from using them because we are too caught up in a High Density Lifestyle. To use the dreaming parts of our mind means we must be FREE; in other words, we have to give the body and mind the chance to relax, be still and listen to the deafening silence of the universe.

The power to dream is something that is innate, just as living a Low Density Lifestyle is innate.

In the Hindu and Buddhist tradition, there is a word, *Buddhi*. It is defined as the enlightened will, awakened mind and discerning intelligence. It comes from the same root Budh, as Buddha. This root word means to be awake: to understand, to know.

Buddhi, the awakened mind, is the highest calling that we can imagine. You don't have to sit for hours on end in meditation to achieve it—it is not that far away. You come into the grasp of buddhi everyday, whether you realize it or not, and whether you are ready or not.

Buddhi is the power to dream and imagine what can be done. It makes formulations for the future, which can be carried out if you choose to. It can imagine big things, stories, adventures and great doings in which the person imagining is the hero or creator. Buddhi is an innate drive—we are born with it and it is encoded in our DNA. It empowers us to dream, to imagine, and to vision, and to do so in the largest way possible; by doing so, buddhi allows us to be FREE.

Over the course of the twentieth century, and into the twenty-first century, there have been a number of people who have inspired us with their words, their actions, their vision and their dreams. These were all people with an incredible facility to dream and imagine; they were all also people who lived a Low Density Lifestyle.

Included in this list are Winston Churchill, Albert Einstein, Buckminster Fuller, Mohandas Gandhi, Vaclav Havel, Helen Keller, John F. Kennedy, Robert F. Kennedy, Martin Luther King Jr., the Dalai Lama, John Lennon, Nelson Mandela, Rosa Parks, Pablo Picasso, Jackie Robinson, Eleanor Roosevelt, Franklin Delano Roosevelt, Dr. Albert Schweitzer, Dr. Benjamin Spock, Mother Teresa and Desmond Tutu.

These people are no different than you or I—we all have the ability to dream. What differs is that they weren't afraid to apply it and use it in the largest way possible, and in doing so, arouse the hopes and dreams of millions.

They put into action their aspirations to better mankind, and in the process inspired many to cultivate their buddhi, and to have the largest vision possible. You may not have such grand ambitions, but their lives are examples of how empowered you can become when you live a Low Density Lifestyle.

Let us look at their words:

> **Winston Churchill:** We make a living by what we get, but we make a life by what we give.

> **Albert Einstein:** The most beautiful thing we can experience is the mysterious. It is the source of all true art and science.

Buckminster Fuller: Everyone is born a genius, but the process of living de-geniuses them.

Mohandas Gandhi: An eye for an eye makes the whole world blind.

Vaclav Havel: Genuine politics—even politics worthy of the name—the only politics I am willing to devote myself to—is simply a matter of serving those around us: serving the community and serving those who will come after us. Its deepest roots are moral because it is a responsibility expressed through action, to and for the whole.

Helen Keller: No pessimist ever discovered the secret of the stars, or sailed to an uncharted land, or opened a new doorway for the human spirit.

John F. Kennedy: The problems of the world cannot possibly be solved by skeptics or cynics whose horizons are limited by the obvious realities. We need men who can dream of things that never were.

Robert F. Kennedy: There are those who look at things the way they are, and ask why. I dream of things that never were, and ask why not?

Martin Luther King, Jr.: Darkness cannot drive out darkness; only light can do that. Hate cannot drive out hate; only love can do that. Hate multiplies hate, violence multiplies violence, and toughness multiplies toughness in a descending spiral of destruction. The chain reaction of evil—hate begetting hate, wars producing more wars—must be broken, or we shall be plunged into the dark abyss of annihilation.

Dalai Lama: With realization of one's own potential and self-confidence in one's ability, one can build a better world.

John Lennon: My role in society, or any artist's or poet's role, is to try and express what we all feel. Not to tell people how to feel. Not as a preacher, not as a leader, but as a reflection of us all.

Nelson Mandela: I learned that courage was not the absence of fear, but the triumph over it. The brave man is not he who does not feel afraid, but he who conquers that fear.

Rosa Parks: I have learned over the years that when one's mind is made up, this diminishes fear; knowing what must be done does away with fear.

Pablo Picasso: The purpose of art is washing the dust of daily life off our souls.

Jackie Robinson: A life is not important except in the impact it has on other lives.

Eleanor Roosevelt: Do what you feel in your heart to be right—for you'll be criticized anyway. You'll be damned if you do, and damned if you don't.

Franklin D. Roosevelt: In our personal ambitions we are individualists. But in our seeking for economic and political progress as a nation, we all go up or else all go down as one people.

Dr. Albert Schweitzer: By having a reverence for life, we enter into a spiritual relation with the world. By practicing reverence for life we become good, deep and alive.

Dr. Benjamin Spock: Happiness is mostly a by-product of doing what makes us feel fulfilled.

Mother Teresa: It is not the magnitude of our actions but the amount of love that is put into them that matters.

Desmond Tutu: If you are neutral in situations of injustice, you have chosen the side of the oppressor. If an elephant has its foot on the tail of a mouse and you say that you are neutral, the mouse will not appreciate your neutrality.

We all are capable of dreaming and using our buddhi, whether it is for the purpose of finding more happiness, more prosperity, a better job, a better relationship, better health, or in making a difference in the lives of others. It is not just a select few who have these qualities. It is not a gift that is rarely parceled out. Each and every one of us has this talent, and each and every one of us has the capacity to cultivate it.

This is the realm of the Low Density Lifestyle, and it beckons and calls your name so that you too can dream the dream of infinite possibilities.

14

Do What You Love

Success is not the key to happiness. Happiness is the key to success. If you love what you are doing, you will be successful.
- Albert Schweitzer

A man is a success if he gets up in the morning and gets to bed at night, and in between he does what he wants to. - Bob Dylan

Follow your bliss and don't be afraid, and doors will open where you didn't know they were going to be. - Joseph Campbell

When you do what you love, you function at a heightened state of awareness, and feel passionate and alive. You work hard, but it will be effortless effort. Life has more meaning when you do what you love, and at these times you feel more in harmony with nature's ebbs and flows, because you are living a Low Density Lifestyle.

What happens when you do something you don't love? Life becomes drudgery and you appear to just go through the motions. There's a certain lack of passion, things feel mechanical and rote, and you wind up losing your sense of joy. At these times you are immersed in a High Density Lifestyle.

To do what you love, you may have to find what that is. Unfortunately for most of us, we are not trained to think in terms of doing what we love, but rather to do what is pragmatic and expedient.

But what that pragmatic thing is may not be what the soul is crying out for you to do. The author Albert Camus once said, "Without work, all life goes rotten. But when work is soulless, life stifles and dies."

You can literally feel it in your bones when what you do doesn't resonate with whom you are. You can actually become physically ill because of the fact that you are living life out of touch with your heartfelt desires and your soul's calling. But if you listen to what your mind, body and soul say, you can start to know who you really are. The universe gives us messages, if we are willing to listen.

The Nobel Laureate Saul Bellow, on speaking of his calling to become a writer, said, "There was a disturbance in my heart, a voice that spoke there and said, I want, I want, I want! It happened every afternoon, and when I tried to suppress it, it got even stronger."

The messages are there, if you are willing to listen and not suppress them. As Saul Bellow pointed out, when you try to suppress the messages, they get stronger. When you try and suppress the messages, what occurs is that the energetic lead shield that gets erected around you when the blockages in the body and mind are extremely dense don't allow the signals that emanate from the Zero-Point Field to reach you.

But when these messages need to get through, they will find a way; that is why people usually use the expression "It was as if I was hit in the head by a hammer" as a manner of describing the way that something finally got through to them.

The messages usually come through loud and clear, but it comes down to, are you willing and ready to listen? Are you willing to live in a Low Density Lifestyle and do what you love? If given the choice, the answer is easy, but in practice, most people don't make the easy choice. That's because fear gets in the way of our acting out our dreams.

"No passion so effectually robs the mind of all its powers of acting and reasoning as fear," Edmund Burke said. Fear can paralyze you and stop you from walking down the path of your true calling. It will make you stay with what is familiar, even if it keeps you living in the heart of a High Density Lifestyle.

But if you feel it in your soul so bad, and know you can't deny what you know to be true, then there is only one option: to pursue it, no matter the obstacles or what may lie ahead. There is no guarantee that pursuing your true calling will lead to instant success (and success usually comes after many years of trying), but if you never try how will you know? And once you open one door, other doors will open and eventually lead you to where you should be.

There is a saying that the journey is the destination. If you listen to the disturbance in your heart, and start on the path of doing what you love, that by itself makes you a success and every step along the way keeps you in the Low Density Lifestyle.

Anybody who has known success knows that they achieved it because they have done what they love. They weren't afraid to fail on their way to achieving that success, because, again, the journey was the destination, and to do what they loved gave them fulfillment all along the way, and made them passionate about achieving their end goal.

Here are some quotes from people who found success by doing what they love. I offer this to you in the hope that it may inspire you to listen to your heart and do what you love.

Miles Davis: Do not fear mistakes. There are none.

Thomas Edison: I have not failed once. I've just found 10,000 ways that didn't work.

Albert Einstein: Anyone who has never made a mistake has never tried anything new.

John W. Gardner: One of the reasons mature people stop learning is that they become less and less willing to risk failure.

Napoleon Hill: Failure is nature's plan to prepare you for great responsibilities.

James Joyce: A man of genius makes no mistakes. His errors are volitional and are the portals of discovery.

John Keats: Failure is in a sense the highway to success, as each discovery of what is false leads us to seek earnestly after what is true.

Robert F. Kennedy: Only those who dare to fail greatly can ever achieve greatly.

Beverly Sills: You may be disappointed if you fail, but you are doomed if you don't try.

Denis Waitley: Chase your passion, not your pension.

Paramahansa Yogananda: The season of failure is the best time for sowing the seeds of success.

15

Connecting to the Spiritual Dimension

The spiritual journey is individual, highly personal. It can't be organized or regulated. It isn't true that everyone should follow one path. Listen to your own truth. - Ram Dass

This force is unlimited. It is always moving and always flowing. The ancient Hawaiians, the Kahunas, used the metaphor of the flow of a running stream to represent the divine force.
– Wayne Dyer

In order to experience everyday spirituality, we need to remember that we are spiritual beings spending some time in a human body.
– Barbara De Angelis

What does it mean to be spiritual, and how does it relate to living a Low Density Lifestyle? When I use the term spiritual, what I mean is living a life that is connected to a divine force, to the pulse of the universe. I have talked about the Zero-Point Field, and it is this field that is the ultimate truth that lies at the heart of the universe.

Some may call this God—and some may give this God a specific name—and some may call it by something else: the Divine Force, Great Spirit, Soul,

Universal Spirit, Universal Mind, Universal Intelligence, Universal Consciousness, etc. However you view this, it is important to understand that there is an underlying force that is at the heart of the universe.

This force is unlimited, infinite, undying and eternal. It is both outside and within us; it is everywhere and in all things. We are connected to it at all times; the less blockages and densities you carry in your body, heart and mind, and the more readily you feel the pulse and flow of the universe within you, then the closer is that connection.

The connection is felt every time you allow yourself to relax, be silent and be still, because it is at these times that the static of unceasing noise that blocks the frequencies and signals that emanate from the Zero-Point Field is quieted. Mother Teresa said:

> We need to find God, and he cannot be found in noise and restlessness. God is the friend of silence. See how nature—trees, flowers, grass—grows in silence; see the stars, the moon and the sun, how they move in silence...We need silence to be able to touch souls.

When you are living a Low Density Lifestyle it is much easier to feel that connection, because the static does not overcome the silence, whereas when living a High Density Lifestyle you will have a hard time feeling that connection, because the static is always there.

People who live a High Density Lifestyle also need a way to find that connection, but unfortunately the way they do so is usually by partaking of things that are detrimental to their health and well-being. They will ingest drugs—pharmaceutical and recreational—and drink excessive amounts of alcohol, all as a means of making themselves numb, getting away from their stresses and trying to feel a connection with something.

In addition, since they have a hard time being still, they will look for the thrill, for something that gives them the buzz and the adrenaline rush, something that has a sense of adventure and risk, all in the name of feeling a connection with something greater than themselves.

Now, I am not saying you shouldn't go and have fun, it's just that some people take it to the extreme. They feel that this is how they make the connection to the force of the universe. Because they are so caught up in the High Density Lifestyle, they don't realize that all they need to do is stop and be still, and within that silence will come the flow that brings forth the pulse of the universe.

Feeling the connection to the spiritual dimension also means holding love in your heart—loving yourself, those close to you, and all the inhabitants of the planet. Love is the ultimate truth at the heart of the universe, and when you feel love in your heart, you create an open energy circuit that connects you to the sacred flow of the universe.

Rumi said, "Your task is not to seek for love, but merely to seek and find all the barriers within yourself that you have built against it." The barriers you have built within yourself that stop you from feeling love are the very same densities and blockages that stop you from living a Low Density Lifestyle. It is so important to surrender and let go of the things that hold you back from feeling love in your heart, because when you do, you can come closer to the Universal Force and be FREE.

There are many ways to feel connected to the spiritual dimension; for some it occurs from attending a church, synagogue, temple or mosque, while for others it is more personal—prayer, meditation, silence, walking in the woods, or some other way.

However you find your method of expression, one thing you need to understand is that spirituality is an everyday affair. You are not just spiritual when you go to church, synagogue, temple or mosque; or when you do the more personal way of expressing your spirituality.

Spirituality, and feeling connected to the spiritual dimension, is something that should be realized at all times. For instance, in the Zen tradition, there is no distinction between spiritual and non-spiritual moments. "Zen does not confuse spirituality with thinking about God while one is peeling potatoes. Zen spirituality is just to peel the potatoes," is a Zen saying.

When that understanding is embedded in every cell of your body, your connection to the spiritual dimension becomes second nature, and all your actions will be directed in that way. You are in the flow and every movement you take and every achievement you make is done with effortless effort.

Part III: Impediments to Living a Low Density Lifestyle

16

Stress

Stress is an ignorant state. It believes that everything is an emergency.
— Natalie Goldberg

For fast-acting relief, try slowing down. — Lily Tomlin

It's not stress that kills us, it is our reaction to it. - Hans Selye

Stress can be quite the destructive force in a person's life, and is both a cause and byproduct of living a High Density Lifestyle.

The term stress was coined by scientist Hans Selye in the 1930s based on his careful observation of physiological responses in laboratory animals. Selye later broadened his findings to include the human response mechanism to a perceived threat, or "stressor."

Selye found that when he exposed various lab animals to unpleasant or harmful stimuli, there were three general stages of reaction. He called these the General Adaptation Syndrome, or GAS. The three stages were Alarm, Resistance and Exhaustion.

By the end of the third stage of GAS, Selye found the animals depleted of their body's most important resources: their adrenal glands were fatigued, their autonomic nervous system was misfiring and their immune systems were burnt out. Furthermore, it was found that this type of reaction played havoc on the feedback loop that constitutes the hypothalamic-pituitary-adrenal axis, the system that controls reactions to stress and regulates many body processes, including digestion, the immune system, mood and emotions, sexuality, and energy storage and expenditure.

Not everyone reacts to stressors in such a detrimental fashion, and there are times when stress can have positive attributes (Selye called stress that enhanced function eustress). But most people don't cope well to stressors because they are on system overload, bombarded by stimuli and overwhelmed by life's demands. Living in this manner is truly a major impediment to a Low Density Lifestyle.

10 warning signs that you are stressed

1. You get sick often. Stress can depress the immune system, making you more susceptible to various upper respiratory ailments.

2. You have digestive problems. One of the places that stress is felt in the body is in the digestive tract. You may have trouble digesting food, you may get stomach pain, you may have acid reflux, or you may have irritable bowel syndrome.

3. You suffer from pain. It could be back pain, joint pain, or even headaches.

4 You easily get anxious. Stress can affect the nervous system and make you very wired, so that things can easily set you off and cause your heart to race, your chest to become tight, and your breathing to become shallow.

5 You are easily angered. Stress will cause you to have a short fuse and to unload on people, even loved ones, often times for reasons quite trivial.

6 You can't sleep. You go to sleep, but your mind is still racing, still thinking about everything. Or you go to sleep, but then you wake up, and can't fall back asleep.

7 You act erratically. You do things impulsively, or you do things that you normally wouldn't do.

8 You are drinking or using recreational drugs a lot. You need a way to unwind, and so you turn to drinking or drugging as an outlet to help you release all that pent up energy.

9 You are using pharmaceutical drugs to enhance/stabilize your mood. Stress can negatively impact your mood, attitude and emotional health, and so if you are not aware of how stressed out you are, you will be turning to prescription drugs to help you.

10 You lack focus and clarity. You forget things easily, and can't think clearly. You also can't focus on any one thing and mentally flit around.

Stress can also lead to weight gain and obesity. There are two main reasons for this. One is behavioral and the other is physiological.

Behaviorally, stressed-out people will often eat even when they're not hungry–this is known as stress eating or emotional eating, and the food choices made are usually not the wisest.

Physiologically, there are a few factors that lead to obesity. One factor is cortisol and cortisol-induced insulin.

When faced with a stressful situation, the body triggers the stress response, the fight-or-flight response. This leads to the secretion of cortisol, adrenaline and other stress hormones along with an increase of blood pressure, breathing and heart rate.

The natural stress response is usually short-term and self-regulating. When the threat is gone, the body returns to normal. As cortisol and adrenaline levels drop, heart rate, respiratory rate and blood pressure, as well as energy levels return to their baseline levels. Other systems inhibited by the stress response return to their regular activities.

The natural stress response goes awry when stress is constant and excessive. In today's society, most people are inundated with overwhelming stress. For those constantly dealing with excessive and chronic stress, the body's fight-or-flight response is constantly on. In turn, the resulting stress hormones released are chronically high.

Chronically high levels of cortisol play a big role in the development of obesity.

Cortisol helps the body handle stress, so when stress goes up, cortisol also goes up. Cortisol stimulates fat and carbohydrate metabolism during stressful situations. This leads to increased blood sugar levels required for fast energy. In turn, this stimulates insulin release, which can lead to an increase in appetite.

When the immediate stress is over, cortisol lingers to help bring the body back into balance after stress. One of the ways it gets things back to balance is by increasing appetite to replace the carbohydrate and fat used for the flight or fight response.

The problem is that in today's society, stress-causing situations—such as traffic jams or computer malfunctions—don't require the body to use up a lot of energy. So, cortisol ends up causing the body to refuel after stress even when it doesn't really need to refuel. This excess fuel or glucose is converted into fat, resulting in increased storage of fat.

What makes matters worse is that cortisol-induced high levels of insulin also leads to increased production and storage of fat. This means that exposure to chronically high levels of cortisol and cortisol-induced insulin are main reasons why stress can lead to an increase in body fat and obesity.

17

Dogma

You can't teach an old dogma new tricks. - Dorothy Parker

Defend your preconceptions with your life. - John Cleese

Don't be trapped by dogma—which is living with the results of other people's thinking. Don't let the noise of others' opinions drown out your own inner voice. And most important, have the courage to follow your heart and intuition. They somehow already know what you truly want to become. Everything else is secondary.
- Steve Jobs

The famed astronomer Galileo learned a very important lesson from Giordano Bruno—namely, to be very careful when questioning dogma, especially when the dogma is set forth by the leading institution of Galileo and Bruno's day, the Catholic Church.

Bruno, a 16th century Renaissance-era scientist, philosopher and poet, and contemporary and colleague of Galileo, was well known in Italy as an author and lecturer of scientific ideas that went against Church doctrine.

His theories caught the attention of the Church, and in 1591 Bruno was arrested and turned over to the Inquisition, on charges of being a heretic. For nine years, Bruno was interrogated, tortured and tried, yet he refused to change his beliefs. Finally, in 1600, he was burned at the stake.

Bruno's horrific fate caused Galileo to express himself a good deal more cautiously on scientific questions in which the Church had a vested interest. By the early 17th century, Galileo was a world-famous scientist, thanks to such developments as his refinement of the telescope, which allowed him to peer into the cosmos and announce Copernicus was right, that the Earth was not the center of the universe. In 1629, he wrote a best-selling book, *Dialogue Concerning the Two Chief World Systems*. In his book, Galileo tried to be fair to both perspectives, and not ruffle too many feathers.

Ultimately, Galileo's enemies within the Inquisition brought charges against him. In 1633 in Rome, he stood to face trial by the Inquisition. As opposed to Bruno, when Galileo was threatened with torture if he did not recant his theories, he acquiesced. For doing so, Galileo's death sentence was commuted to house arrest for the rest of his life.

The incident of the Inquisition represents one of the worst examples of dogmatic and inflexible behavior in recorded history. In fact, it wasn't until 1992, on the 350th anniversary of Galileo's death, that Pope John Paul II finally apologized to Galileo for his treatment by the Inquisition. In regards to Bruno, in the late 19th century a statue was erected at the site of his death in honor of the cause of free thought. And in the year 2000, 400 years after his execution, official expression of "profound sorrow" and acknowledgement of error at Bruno's condemnation to death was made, again by Pope John Paul II.

We all carry dogmas, those things that we hold onto dearly, whether they are right or wrong, and whether they fly in the face of reason or not. Most people will defend their dogmas to their death, if need be.

Dogmas are directly related to the desire to control your life and the lives of others. They are deeply held beliefs that reinforce the way you see the world. They are illogical and unreasonable, and yet are so ingrained and embedded in the subconscious that you are not even aware that they are your guiding force.

Dogmas cause us to become rigid in our beliefs, and lead us to a sense of absolutism, that it's my way or the highway. Dogmas lead to knee-jerk, reflexive reactions that may not be in your best interest.

When you are inflexible in your thinking and unyielding in your beliefs, even in the face of being shown you are wrong, both body and mind become rigid. This is a sure-fire way to find yourself in a High Density Lifestyle, because you are not capable of letting go of belief patterns, and this holding pattern will lead to an increasing buildup of densities in the body.

Here is an exercise to do: ask yourself, What are three dogmas that I live by? Don't ponder too long over it; instead just write down what quickly comes to mind. Once you can start to identify your dogmas and bring them to your conscious mind, you can start to understand them and how they guide you and dictate, without your knowing, the decisions you make, the way you think, the people you associate with and all other facets of your life.

Dogmas are the byproduct of the need to control. They are our modus operandi, the backbone of our rigid thinking, and an impediment to our ability to be FREE and live a Low Density Lifestyle. They cause us to be stuck in patterns and habits that are detrimental to our well-being.

Dogmas affect both our physical and emotional health. A person that holds onto dogmas is a person who is subject to rigid thinking, and rigid thinking can lead to rigidity and pain in the body and mind.

Dr. John Sarno is well known as the author of a number of best-selling books, including *Healing Back Pain* and *The Mind-Body Prescription*. In his books he articulates his belief that most back and other chronic pain is caused by suppressed emotions, including anger, guilt, anxiety, depression and low self-esteem. I would say that all those emotions could be put into the category of rigid thinking, because when we wallow in our own emotions and get stuck in them, we do not give the body and mind the ability to just let go and be free and flexible. Holding onto emotions, whatever that emotion might be, creates a holding pattern in the body.

Sarno calls the pain that is created by this holding pattern "Tension Myositis Syndrome," and he has had tremendous success treating chronic pain using his approach. His method focuses on teaching people to become more aware and mindful of their thinking and living habits—this can help the person recognize when habits and actions derive from dogmas.

Dogmas cause us to see the world through a narrow lens, and to perceive that the universe centers around our ego. By believing that the world operates in this manner, we become more reflexive in our response to the actions of others.

Being continually reflexive as a response mechanism will cause you to never get past yourself. Your buttons will constantly be pushed because things will always appear as a personal attack and you will always be on the defensive.

It will be impossible to achieve a Low Density Lifestyle when dogmas run your life. You will be too busy defending your preconceptions with every cell in your body and unable to allow ideas and thoughts to enter your being that may run counter to everything you hold dear to your heart.

Dogmas cause you to see the world in black and white terms, and keep you staying firm in the belief that you are right and others are wrong.

But the world does not operate in purely black and white terms. Most of life is shaded with grey, and these are the areas that cannot be predicted or controlled. Dogmas want everything to be tidy and summed up easily. They do not like messiness.

But to be human is to be messy and complicated. Life is messy, human emotions are messy, and human relationships are messy. All is messy and complicated. There is no getting around that.

The way to deal with the messy and complicated life we all live is to learn to become fluid and flexible of mind and body, to let go of the desire to control and learn to flow, to be like water. As the old saying goes, "You can't stop the waves, but you can learn to surf."

Again, ask yourself, What are three dogmas that I live by? Write them down on paper and then examine them, and ask yourself why do I hold onto them? What is so important about the dogma that I must hold onto it? The first step in letting go of habits is to become aware of them, so becoming aware of the dogmas that dictate your life is step number one.

If you want to take this exercise one step further, after writing down the three dogmas (and you don't have to stop at three), play a little word association. Look at the first dogma you have written down, and then quickly jot down five to ten different words or phrases that immediately come to mind in relation to that dogma. What you come up with may seem related or it may not. The key is to not spend too much time thinking, and instead to just write down whatever comes to mind. Your answers may surprise you.

The more you become aware of your dogmas, the more mindful you become about how these deeply embedded patterns rule your life. And as you ponder these dogmas and understand them better, the more you will be able to become free of them.

As I said, life is messy and complicated, and as a consequence our actions may at times be messy and complicated, which means we most probably will never be perfect. That is one of the consequences of letting go of our dogmas—you come to realize that you are imperfect. Perfectionists please take note of this.

Although our actions may never be perfect, by becoming more aware and mindful of them, you will be able to note when you are doing things that are not in the best interest of ourselves and others, and when you are doing things that are rooted in deeply held preconceptions and dogmas.

As you become more mindful and aware of your actions, the more likely it is that you can get off of the toxic merry-go-round that is the High Density Lifestyle.

18

Resistance to New Ideas

Don't worry about people stealing your ideas. If your ideas are any good, you'll have to ram them down people's throats. - Howard Aiken

The human body has two ends on it: one to create with and one to sit on. Sometimes people get their ends reversed. When this happens they need a kick in the seat of the pants.
- Roger von Oech

Truth is violently opposed before it is accepted as self evident.
- Arthur Schopenhauer

When you live a Low Density Lifestyle, you are capable of thinking more creatively and coming up with new and progressive ideas, because as I explained in Chapter 13, your mind becomes open to the infinite creative pulse of the Zero-Point Field.

When you live a High Density Lifestyle, you are prone to dogmatic, inflexible and rigid thinking, as I just explained in the previous chapter. What happens in this case is that you have an inherent resistance to new ideas and your knee-jerk reaction is to reflexively dismiss them.

There is a biological reason for why most people categorically reject new and innovate ideas. Anatomically, our brain shares certain functions with other mammals. The lowest part of the brain is the brainstem, also called the R-complex, Reptilian complex or Reptilian brain.

It is so-named because it is the part of the brain that humans and reptiles share. The R-complex is responsible for certain instinctive and destructive responses, including rage, xenophobia, and survival. The R-Complex can override the more rational functions of the brain and result in unpredictable, primitive and violent behavior in both reptiles and humans. It is also the part of the brain that gets overtaxed when you are living a High Density Lifestyle.

When a reptile confronts something new and different, its R-complex mobilizes into action and causes the reptile to respond in one of three ways:

1) It attacks it;
2) It kills it and eats it; or
3) It runs away from it

When humans are presented with something new and different, such as a new idea, they too are capable of a reptilian response: they can reject the idea by either attacking it, killing it or running away from it. This is the challenge for people living a Low Density Lifestyle—their new ideas can trigger the reptilian response in those living a High Density Lifestyle.

But for those living a Low Density Lifestyle, if you believe in your idea and your vision with all your heart, it will prevail. The British politician Tony Benn put it well when he said, "It's the same each time with progress. First they ignore you, then they say you're mad, then dangerous, then there's a pause and then you can't find anyone who disagrees with you."

And Warren Bennis, the best-selling author, organizational consultant and founder of The Leadership Institute at the University of Southern California, said, "Innovation—any new idea—by definition will not be accepted at first. It takes repeated attempts, endless demonstrations, and monotonous rehearsals before innovation can be accepted and internalized by an organization. This requires courageous patience."

The reason it requires courageous patience for a new idea to gain hold is because of the resistance to new ideas that occurs amongst those who live a High Density Lifestyle.

Many a brilliant idea has been rejected, shot down by so-called experts because they believed they knew better. But because the people who came up with these ideas were creative thinkers and visionaries living a Low Density Lifestyle, and believed in the power of their ideas, they were able to overcome the entrenched way of thinking of the experts and bring their ideas to fruition.

As I show from the following examples, you are in good company if others reject your progressive vision and idea. I encourage you to read the following list and use it to inspire yourself to stay strong in your heart with what you believe to be true.

Brilliant Ideas—But Rejected by the Experts

Apple Computer

"So we went to Atari and said, 'Hey, we've got this amazing thing, even built with some of your parts, and what do you think about funding us? Or we'll give it to you. We just want to do it. Pay our salary, we'll come work for you.' And they said, 'No.' So then we went to Hewlett-Packard, and they said, 'Hey, we don't need you. You haven't got through college yet.'"—Apple Computer Inc. founder Steve Jobs on attempts to get Atari and H-P interested in his and Steve Wozniak's personal computer.

Federal Express

Fred Smith, while a student at Yale, came up with the concept of Federal Express, a national overnight delivery service. The U.S. Postal Service, U.P.S., his own business professor, and virtually every delivery expert in the United States predicted his enterprise would fail. Based on their experiences in the industry, no one, they said, would pay a fancy price for speed and reliability.

Fred Astaire

"Can't act. Can't sing. Balding. Can dance a little."—M-G-M executive, reacting to Fred Astaire's screen test, 1928

Gone With the Wind

1) "Forget it, Louis, no Civil War picture ever made a nickel."—Irving Thalberg's warning to Louis B. Mayer regarding *Gone With the Wind*

2) "I'm just glad it'll be Clark Gable who's fallin' on his face and not Gary Cooper."—Gary Cooper, turning down lead in *Gone With The Wind*

John Elway

"He'll never be any good."—Robert Irsay, owner of the Baltimore Colts, after trading newly drafted quarterback John Elway to the Denver Broncos, 1983

The Beatles

"We don't like their sound, and guitar music is on the way out." —Decca Recording Co. rejecting the Beatles, 1962

Mrs. Fields Cookies

"A cookie store is a bad idea. Besides, the market research reports say

America likes crispy cookies, not soft and chewy cookies like you make."—Response to Debbi Fields' idea of starting Mrs. Fields' Cookies.

Tollbooth Collecting

In 1959 a man living in Marin County, California, and working in San Francisco, devised a method to reduce his commuting time. He was tired of being stuck every day in his car because of the tollbooths on either side of the Golden Gate Bridge. There must be a way to save time, fuel consumption, and wear and tear on the vehicles, he thought. He came up with a revolutionary idea: why not have toll collectors on one side of the bridge and let the toll be double the one-way fare? In this day and age that would hardly be considered a radical concept. However, in 1959 it had never been done before, and no one was sure if it was such a good idea. It flew in the face of common practice. The critical thinkers were able to tear apart the idea and find the errors inherent in it. It wasn't until 1967, eight years later, that the idea was given a trial run. A new regional commissioner of transportation had been appointed, and since he was somewhat of a neophyte, he was not totally aware of all the "accepted" practices. He was willing to give it a shot and did. It was such a phenomenal success that within one year, bridge toll collecting across the country adopted the practice.

Handwashing for Doctors

In the mid-1800s in Vienna, Dr. Ignaz Semmelweis, an obstetrician, proposed that obstetricians wash their hands before delivering babies to lessen the possibility of spreading disease. He even proved his point by doing a study that showed how washing hands would lessen disease in newborns. The physicians involved refused to believe his idea could make a difference and ran him out of Vienna. He ended up committing suicide as a result of the emotional stress he suffered.

The Telephone

1) In 1861, in Germany, Phillip Reiss invented a machine that could transmit music and was on the verge of inventing the telephone, but was persuaded there was no market for a telephone, because the telegraph was an adequate way to send messages. Fifteen years later Alexander Graham Bell invented the telephone.

2) "What use could the company make of an electric toy?"—Western Union, when it turned down rights to the telephone in 1878.

Xerox

In 1938 Chester Carlson invented xerography. Virtually every major corporation, including IBM and Xerox, didn't think much of his idea and rejected it. They felt that since carbon paper was cheap and readily available, no one would buy an expensive copying machine.

U.S. Patent Office

In 1899 Charles Duell, the director of the U.S. Patent Office, suggested that the government close the office because everything that could be invented had been invented.

The Radio

"The wireless music box has no imaginable commercial value. Who would pay for a message sent to nobody in particular?"—David Sarnoff's associates in rejecting a proposal for investment in the radio in the 1920s.

Talking Pictures

"Who the hell wants to hear actors talk?"—H.M. Warner (Warner Brothers) before rejecting proposal for movies with sound in 1927.

The Airplane
"Heavier-than-air flying machines are impossible."—Lord Kelvin, president, Royal Society, 1895.

Nautilus Machines
"You want to have consistent and uniform muscle development across all of your muscles? It can't be done. It's just a fact of life. You just have to accept inconsistent muscle development as an unalterable condition of weight training."—Rejection letter to Arthur Jones, who invented the Nautilus Fitness Machine.

The Computer
"I think there is a world market for maybe five computers."—Thomas Watson, chairman of IBM, 1943.

The Personal Computer
"There is no reason anyone would want a computer in their home."—Ken Olsen, president, chairman and founder of Digital Equipment Corp., 1977.

Women's Suffrage
"Sensible and responsible women do not want to vote."—Grover Cleveland, 1905.

Tapping the Atom
"There is no likelihood man can ever tap the power of the atom."—Robert Miliham, Nobel Prize in Physics, 1923

Babe Ruth
"Ruth made a big mistake when he gave up pitching."—Tris Speaker, 1921

The Automobile

"The horse is here today, but the automobile is only a novelty—a fad."—President of Michigan Savings Bank advising against investing in the Ford Motor Company.

The Television

"Video won't be able to hold on to any market it captures after the first six months. People will soon get tired of staring at a plywood box every night." —Daryl F. Zanuck, 20th Century Fox, commenting on television in 1946.

19

Control and Fear

Men are not prisoners of fate, but only prisoners of their own minds.
— Franklin D. Roosevelt

The one permanent emotion of man is fear—fear of the unknown, the complex, the inexplicable. What he wants above everything else is safety. - H. L. Mencken

The hens they all cackle, the roosters all beg,
But I will not hatch, I will not hatch.
For I hear all the talk of pollution and war
As the people all shout and the airplane roar,
So I'm staying in here where it's safe and it's warm,
And I WILL NOT HATCH! - Shel Silverstein

The human brain is estimated to have one trillion brain cells.

We are capable of storing 280 quintillion—280,000,000,000,000,000,000—bits of memory in our brain.

The speed of our brain is estimated to range from 100 to 100,000 teraflops (a teraflop is one trillion flops, and a flop is the standard measure of computing speed). The world's fastest computer operates at a speed of 100 billion flops.

We process 125 bits of data per second through our conscious mind. The unconscious mind processes billions of data per second. And our memory approaches a 100% retention rate. We remember potentially everything, although most of those memories lie in the unconscious.

And yet, researchers into human potential tell us that we use at most five percent of our mind's capabilities, and some researchers believe that most people use no more than one percent.

How can this be? The human brain is the greatest computer ever built, and yet we barely tap into its incredible potential. Instead we stay within our narrow comfort zone of habits, which cause us to barely scratch the surface of what we are capable of. Because of this, we are held back from the ability to achieve a Low Density Lifestyle, and with it our inalienable rights of health, happiness, prosperity and fulfillment.

We are trapped in a feedback loop of negativity and stress, and the primary cause of this is fear: Fear of the unknown, fear of change, fear of venturing into something outside the comfort zone, fear of an inability to control, and fear of unpredictability, turbulence and chaos. This way of being makes you fearful of being in the flow, and as you have learned by now, leads you straight into the path of a High Density Lifestyle.

From the day you are born to the day you die, it is embedded in your body, mind and soul that this is a world you must control, and by so doing you can live a predictable and secure life with minimal hassles, headaches and crises that will upset the apple cart.

In order to maintain control over all things you must then become a mega-control freak. Everything needs to be orderly, routine and scheduled down to the last minute; and you need to compartmentalize and fit everything into predictable patterns. When you find what your niche is, once you are comfortable with that niche, you tenaciously guard it with your life, if need be.

The famed Peter Principle is a prime example of this. *The Peter Principle* is the title of a bestselling business book originally published in 1968, by psychologist and educator Laurence J. Peter.

The Peter Principle states that most organizations rise to the level of their incompetence, and explains why boredom, bungling and bad management are built into every organization. The theory is that employees within an organization will advance to their highest level of competence and then be promoted to and remain at a level at which they are incompetent. Dr. Peter's book shows how America's corporate career track drives employees relentlessly upward—until they get promoted into jobs they just can't do and wind up desperately treading water, driving their colleagues crazy and dragging down productivity and profit.

The reason the Peter Principle is a fact of life is that, as I said above, once you find your niche, you will then tenaciously guard it with your life. Once we have control over our domain, our little fiefdom, we will hold steady as Lord and Master of our Domain.

If you work for an organization and show mastery of your fiefdom, then the company will want to promote you, whether you are ready or not to go past your niche. As the Peter Principle so aptly states, most people are not capable of going beyond their position, and so the organization becomes weighted down with employees who do not know what they are doing. This is bureaucracy in action—it is what happens in most bureaucracies.

I see this all the time in my work as an integrative medicine health provider. Most people I consult with have a very hard time letting go of habits that are affecting their health in a detrimental way. For most people I have to tread lightly and gently encourage them to make changes. I have found for many people that change needs to be slow and incremental, because for many people change can be so very painful.

In my clinical practice, if I notice that a patient has this type of temperament, I give them homework that is simple and easily attainable. I ask that everyday they do one thing different from their usual routine. If they always brush their teeth with their right hand, I suggest they do so with their left. If they always drive the same route to work, I advise them to drive a different way. I ask them to make a note of what they did different each day, and to show it to me the next time I see them.

For most of the people who are assigned this task, they find it to be fun, and it helps them to see how stuck in a rut they really are. Once they get the wheels in motion, doing one different thing a day helps them to be much more at ease with breaking out of their many long-held habits.

Yet some patients are not able to come to grips with the task. The usual sequence that follows for these folks is that when they come back in they say they left the journal listing the different things they've done either at home or in the car. The excuses will go on for a few visits, and then they stop coming in altogether. The termination of their treatments tells me that even one change a day is one change a day too many and too difficult for them to achieve.

And these are the people who are willing to consider that they have to make changes in order to develop better health. As popular as integrative medicine has become, it is still a small segment of our population that visits an integrative health provider. Most people continue with the usual routine when they are sick—visiting their doctor, who then will write a prescription for a drug. This is a painless way to deal with your health, because you don't have to go outside your comfort zone and make changes.

The story of the famed philosopher Jiddhu Krishnamurti is a very instructive one in this regard. Born in 1895 in Madanapalle, India, in 1909, Krishnamurti met C.W. Leadbeater of the Theosophical Society, who believed the young boy to be the coming "World Teacher." He was subsequently raised, educated and prepared for his role under the tutelage of Leadbeater and Annie Besant, leaders of the Society at the time.

But in 1929, Krishnamurti broke free of the organization and disavowed his appointment as the World Teacher. On August 3 of that year he gave a speech announcing to all his followers that he was no longer interested in being their Messiah.

Krishnamurti said in part:

> I do not want followers, and I mean this. The moment you follow someone you cease to follow Truth. I am not concerned whether you pay attention to what I say or not. I want to do a certain thing in the world and I am going to do it with unwavering concentration. I am concerning myself with only one essential thing: to set man free. I desire to free him from all cages, from all fears, and not to found religions, new sects, nor to establish new theories and new philosophies.

Krishnamurti's followers were in shock by his proclamation, which took them totally by surprise. His followers then fell into three general camps: there were those who suffered nervous breakdowns, because they had so much invested in Krishnamurti as World Teacher that for him to tell them something that was such a radical departure from what they were used to hearing was just too much for them to bear; there were those who turned on him, and did everything in their power to subvert his work; and there were those who were inspired by his words, and used Krishnamurti's new teachings as an impetus to cultivate the ability to become truly free.

Krishnamurti's biographer, Mary Lutyens, wrote of the incident, "After all the years of proclaiming the Coming, of stressing over and over again the danger of rejecting the World Teacher when he came because he was bound to say something wholly new and unexpected, something contrary to most people's preconceived ideas and hopes, the leaders of Theosophy, one after the other, fell into the trap against which they had so unremittingly warned others."

From that point on in his writings and his lectures, until his death at the age of 90, Jiddhu Krishnamurti was relentless in his denouncing of all organized belief, the notion of "gurus", and the whole teacher-follower relationship. Instead he was single minded in his dedication to the work of setting man absolutely, totally free.

What would happen if we let go of our desire to control? We would have to allow for the unknown, for unpredictability, and for chaos to enter into our lives. That is not to say that we must throw caution to the wind and live a completely tumultuous existence—we all need a fair amount of order in our lives. But chaos is also a part of our lives.

For most folks, unpredictability and chaos is a blight to be avoided at all costs, because when it happens it is a shock to the system. But the reality is that this is a world of chaos, unpredictability and change. It is said that the only thing constant in life is change.

In life, there is a dance that is done between order and chaos, and it is this: order arises from chaos. This is actually a scientific truth. Whenever you are in the midst of chaos, when the swirls of uncertainty seem overwhelming, if you hold steady order will eventually be established. And like the phoenix that rises from the ashes, the order that arises will be a new order, one that will take you to new ways of seeing, thinking and living.

Chaos is your friend. Order is also, so it would behoove you to embrace both of them. And when chaos does show up—and invariably it will, sooner or later—if you open your mind to new possibilities, you won't be disappointed.

The late Gilda Radner once said:

> I wanted a perfect ending. Now I've learned, the hard way, that some poems don't rhyme, and some stories don't have a clear beginning, middle, and end. Life is about not knowing, having to change, taking the moment and making the best of it, without knowing what's going to happen next. Delicious Ambiguity.

So when you let go of your desire to control, you let go of your fears, because no longer will you fear the unknown. No longer will the unknown be seen as something that can wreak havoc on you. Instead it will be seen as something that can bring you to a greater level of understanding of what it truly means to be a human being. And this is the ultimate destiny of living a Low Density Lifestyle.

20

Poor Diet, Poor Health

A crust eaten in peace is better than a banquet partaken in anxiety.
– Aesop, Fables

Eating a vegetarian diet, walking (exercising) everyday, and meditating is considered radical. Allowing someone to slice your chest open and graft your leg veins in your heart is considered normal and conservative. – Dean Ornish

The appearance of a disease is swift as an arrow; its disappearance slow, like a thread.
– Chinese Proverb

A poor diet, high in fast foods, junk foods, processed foods, transfats and saturated fats is not conducive to good health. Over time, eating this way can lead to obesity, diabetes, cardiovascular disorders, cancer and other types of chronic, autoimmune and degenerative conditions. In other words, eating a poor diet will lead a person straight down the path of a High Density Lifestyle.

A person eating a poor diet is taxing their body to no end, and people who live and function in this manner are usually on a number of medications. But taking drugs is not the answer to achieving better health—at best they are a band-aid, used to cover up the symptoms but incapable of getting at the root.

Poor diet and poor health are huge impediments to living a Low Density Lifestyle. People in this situation are trapped in quicksand, stuck in a quagmire that is robbing them of their health, their vitality and their full potential as human beings.

In September 2004 the medical journal *The Lancet* published a study that had followed 30,000 men and women on six continents. The conclusion of the study was that changing lifestyle could prevent at least 90% of all heart disease.

Eating a poor diet creates inflammation in the body, which can then lead to chronic disease. Junk foods, high-fat meats, processed foods, sugar, high fructose corn syrup, artificial sweeteners, and fast foods all will increase inflammation in your body. This is partially due to the unhealthy fats used in preparing and processing these foods, especially trans fats and saturated fats. Processed meats such as lunchmeats, hot dogs and sausages contain chemicals such as nitrites that are associated with increased inflammation and chronic disease.

Saturated fats are also found in meats, dairy products and eggs. These foods also contain fatty acids called arachidonic acid. While some arachidonic acid is essential for your health, too much arachidonic acid in the diet may make your inflammation worse.

Living an unhealthy lifestyle, a High Density Lifestyle, is no way to exist. This way of life is full of karmic imbalance; there is only one way to escape, and that is to go towards the path of health and wellness.

21

The Curse of Knowledge

*I was born not knowing and have only had a
little time to change that here and there.
— Richard Feynman*

*If stock market experts were so expert,
they would be buying stock, not selling advice.
— Norman R. Augustine*

*If the world should blow itself up, the last audible voice would be
that of an expert saying it can't be done. — Peter Ustinov*

The Greek philosopher Epictetus said, "It is impossible for a man to learn what he thinks he already knows." When a person becomes extremely knowledgeable in an area, to the point that they become a specialist in a field, their ability to be flexible in their thinking lessens, because they lose a certain degree of open-mindedness.

Andrew S. Grove, the co-founder of Intel, said, "When everybody knows that something is so, it means that nobody knows nothing." Once a person becomes an authority figure, it's easy for the blinders to go up and cause them to reject anything that doesn't fit into their frame of knowledge.

This is known as the curse of knowledge. The phrase was first used in a 1989 paper in *The Journal of Political Economy*, but the understanding of the stifling effect of too much specialization goes back far beyond the journal article.

Living a Low Density Lifestyle keeps you from gaining a foothold in the curse of knowledge, because you maintain a fluidity and suppleness of mind and body and don't become so enamored of your beliefs and convince yourself that you are an expert. It is only when you are living a High Density Lifestyle will that occur.

In the Zen tradition, one of the more valuable lessons taught is the importance of maintaining a beginner's mind, a mind open to new possibilities, and not allow the mind to become cluttered with the smug sense of authority. The Zen master Shunryu Suzuki said, "In the beginner's mind there are many possibilities, but in the expert's mind there are few."

The curse of knowledge creates experts who believe they know everything about everything about their field of expertise. The media look to them as the opinion makers, and they become the thought leaders in the field—even though they usually are wrong more often than right. Not only are those who are looked up to by the media and general public invariably wrong most of the time, these folks also are basing their pontificating from the perspective of a High Density Lifestyle.

The worst thing a person can do is become so smug and satisfied with their knowledge that they think they know everything about a given topic—if they are doing that, you know they are living a High Density Lifestyle.

An important trait of living a Low Density Lifestyle is maintaining beginner's mind and keeping a sense of curiosity and openness, so that you never fall into the trap of the curse of knowledge.

Christopher Cerf and Victor Navasky, the founders of the Institute for Expertology, and authors of *The Experts Speak* and *Mission Accomplished! (or How We Won the War in Iraq)*, have spent many years researching the curse of knowledge. Having done much scholarly study in the field of Expertology, they have found that, "The iron law of Expertology is that the experts are never right." They have compiled statements made by the experts, who, suffering from the curse of knowledge, made proclamations that turned out to be very, very wrong. Here are just a few of them:

> "I think children belong with their mother." —O.J. Simpson, to television correspondent David Jackson, that prosecutor Christopher Darden should not be granted custody of his 3-month old daughter.—Reported in *Newsweek*, September 1, 1997.

> "The message of October, 1987, should not be taken lightly. The great bull market is over." —Robert R. Prechter, in *Business Week*, November 30, 1987.

> "The one thing I won't let happen to me is I won't let a ball go through my legs." —Bill Buckner, Boston Red Sox first baseman, promising that chronic pain in his legs would not affect his fielding during

the 1986 World Series, which the Red Sox proceeded to lose as a direct result of Buckner's allowing a ground ball to roll through his legs (October 1986).

"Among the really difficult problems of the world, [the Arab-Israeli conflict is] one of the simplest and most manageable." —Walter Lippmann, newspaper column (April 27, 1948).

"Statistics show that teen pregnancy drops off significantly after age 25." —Mary Anne Tebedo, Member of the Colorado State Senate, Remark on the Senate floor during the 1995 Session (May 14, 1995).

"God himself could not sink this ship." —A deckhand on the Titanic, 1912.

"If excessive smoking actually plays a role in the production of lung cancer, it seems to be a minor one." —Dr. W. C. Heuper, National Cancer Institute, 1954.

"All the waste in a year from a nuclear power plant can be stored under a desk." —Ronald Reagan, 1980.

"Approximately 80% of our air pollution stems from hydrocarbons released by vegetation. So let's not go overboard in setting and enforcing tough emissions standards for man-made sources." —Ronald Reagan, 1980.

"If the motion of the earth were circular, it would be violent and contrary to nature, and could not be eternal, since nothing violent is eternal. It follows, therefore, that the earth is not moved with a circular motion." —St. Thomas Aquinas, 1270.

"Major combat operations in Iraq have ended. In the battle of Iraq, the United States and our allies have prevailed." —President George W. Bush, May 1, 2003.

"Military action will not last more than a week." —Bill O'Reilly, *The O'Reilly Factor*, January 23, 2003, discussing the upcoming war in Iraq.

Part IV: What a Low Density Lifestyle Can Do For You

22

Health and Longevity

*Healing may not be so much about getting better,
as about letting go of everything that isn't you—all of the
expectations, all of the beliefs—and becoming who you are.
— Rachel Naomi Remen*

*Most people think that aging is irreversible and we know that
there are mechanisms even in the human machinery that allow for the
reversal of aging, through correction of diet, through anti-oxidants,
through removal of toxins from the body, through exercise, through
yoga and breathing techniques, and through meditation.
- Deepak Chopra*

*In minds crammed with thoughts, organs clogged with toxins, and
bodies stiffened with neglect, there is just no space for anything else.
- Alison Rose Levy, "An Ancient Cure for Modern Life,"
Yoga Journal, Jan/Feb 2002*

One of the best side effects of living a Low Density Lifestyle is that you'll feel better. By eating a better diet, incorporating movement into your life, cultivating your emotional well-being, being more flexible in your thinking habits, being less stressed and more relaxed, being more empowered about your health choices, and following other precepts of a Low Density Lifestyle, your immune system will be stronger and more capable of keeping you healthy.

When you are living a Low Density Lifestyle you are more in the flow, and when this is the case you have the capability of experiencing optimal health. In Chinese Medicine and Acupuncture, it is said that good health comes about when the qi, the life force energy, is flowing unimpeded through the body, and illness comes into being when the qi is blocked and the flow is interrupted in the body.

One of the benefits of feeling better is that it can allow you to reduce or eliminate the need to take medications. The amount of medications people take nowadays is out of control, having skyrocketed in recent years. In 2008, total sales in the U.S. for prescription drugs were $291.5 billion, with a national average of 11.5 prescriptions filled per person. The number one selling drug is Lipitor, a statin used for cholesterol, and the next two most popular drugs are Nexium, for acid reflux, and Plavix, used to reduce the risk of heart attack and stroke. In 2008, anti-depressants formed the next category of best-selling drugs, with $9.5 billion in annual sales.

Most people are programmed to run to their doctor and take a drug at the slightest outbreak of trouble. The amount of drug advertising in the media is a good part of the reason why people are programmed to think this way—over $4 billion for TV ads and $1 billion for online marketing were spent in 2008. That kind of money buys a lot of influence, and it's because of this that we've become so far removed from utilizing our body's own healing mechanisms.

It is impossible to develop and cultivate good health when you take prescription drugs—they are not the answer to creating health. Now, I'm not necessarily saying don't take any drugs, nor am I saying that you should immediately stop what you're taking. I am saying that if you take medications you need to reflect on what your health goals are. In other words, to become healthy you need to figure out an exit strategy for getting off medications, and to formulate an exit strategy you need to become proactive about your health.

You can never become truly healthy when you rely on drugs, because they are taxing and toxic on the body. They also block the ability of our innate natural healing system to function, and it is the innate healing system that is at the root of creating true health. The key to developing better health is in cultivating the power of the innate healing system. Unfortunately, modern medicine places no value on the innate healing system, and instead puts its faith in drugs.

Norman Cousins, the author of the best-selling book *Anatomy of an Illness*, which detailed his recovery from a terminal illness by harnessing the power of his innate healing system, put it well when he said:

> There is such a thing as a healing system. Unfortunately, the healing system is not part of a great deal of medical education. In medical textbooks, for example, you're not going to find very much in the index under healing system. You'll find listings for all the other systems but none for the healing system. And that unfortunately is an accurate indicator that the healing system is not sufficiently appreciated or understood. Yet if 85 percent of all illnesses are self-limiting, something must be happening, and that something should have a name. I'm pretty sure that healing

> system is about the best we can come up with, but why isn't it taught as such?...We spend so much time getting to know bugs that we've lost sight of people.

This is another reason why you need to be empowered and proactive about your health—so that you can cultivate and utilize the power of the healing system that lies within each one of us.

Ultimately, to tap into the innate healing system, you have to, as the quote from Rachel Naomi Remen stated at the beginning of this chapter, "let go of everything that isn't you." Letting go of everything that isn't you entails letting go of all the high density in your body, mind and spirit that are blocking you from being who you truly are.

When you let go of your density, you are not only tapping into the body's innate healing system, but you are tapping into the most powerful source of healing energy in the universe—the Zero-Point Field. When the mind is in the flow state and communicates with the Zero-Point Field, the mind is capable of thinking in a more visionary and far-reaching capacity; and when the body accesses the Zero-Point Field, the body is capable of healing in a profound way. This is known as quantum healing, distance healing, or spiritual healing.

Traditional healers have always been aware of this. The late Papa Henry Auwae, a master of traditional Hawaiian medicines said, "Medicine is 80% spiritual and 20% medicine."

Letting go of everything can never happen to those living a High Density Lifestyle, and so it is extremely difficult for people living this way to experience profound healing. It becomes a vicious circle, because people living a High Density Lifestyle generally don't feel well and will take assorted medications, yet taking medications will keep you on the path of living a High Density Lifestyle.

Just as a person living a High Density Lifestyle will have densities and blockages measurably seen in their blood chemistry in the form of high blood pressure, along with high levels of plaque, cholesterol, triglycerides and other negative determinants, someone living a Low Density Lifestyle will have blood values that are a reflection of someone in excellent health. And how can someone not be in outstanding health if they experience flow in their everyday life?

By living in this manner and experiencing exceptional health, it increases the odds of longevity many times over. Studies of cultures that are known for longevity have found certain common attributes, and many of these traits are the recommended lifestyle characteristics of a Low Density Lifestyle. These traits include:

- Eating a simple, whole foods, plant-based diet
- Eating less, not more
- Being active, and moving in ways that accentuate flow
- Making quiet time and also making time to relax, unwind, destress, decompress and nap
- Being happy and having a joyful approach to life
- Exercising your mind and having a purpose in life
- Maintaining a connection to the spiritual dimension of life

Living by these traits increases the odds of your living a long and healthy life, full of vitality, happiness and fulfillment. And what more could you ask for?

23

Happiness and Joy

If you want to be happy, be. - Leo Tolstoy

*Happiness is when what you think, what you say,
and what you do are in harmony.
- Mohandas Gandhi*

*I have no name: I am but two days old. What shall I call thee?
I happy am, Joy is my name. Sweet joy befall thee! - William Blake*

What brings about happiness and joy is different for every individual. But there are certain keys to creating happiness, and these are the twelve steps to living a Low Density Lifestyle. If you are doing what you love, life has meaning and purpose; one of the biggest stressors in life is having a job that is pure drudgery. When you are doing something you love, you wake up every morning feeling energetic and raring to go.

When you feel healthy, when you feel flexible of body and mind, when you remember to laugh, when you allow yourself to dream and use your creativity, your are firing on all cylinders and living a more fulfilling life.

Granted, life is not always a bed of roses, and there will always be bumps and bruises along the way that can leave you feeling dejected, beaten and jaded, but when you live a Low Density Lifestyle, you won't feel overtaken and overwhelmed by negative circumstances, and instead will remember that ultimately, life is a vital and vibrant journey through the calm winds and tempestuous storms that are weathered over time.

Happiness is a choice, and also a learned skill. It's easy to get into a negative frame of mind on a regular basis; most people, because they are living a High Density Lifestyle, are unhappy and are more than willing to share their unhappiness with others. There is also much going on in the world that can leave you feeling unhappy, frustrated and fearful.

But you can still be happy amidst all the negativity around you. And the happiness you experience will not be a Pollyanna-type one, where you stay oblivious to what is going on about you and proceed to live in your own world.

Medications are certainly not required to be happy. As I stated in the previous chapter, in 2008 anti-depressants had sales in the U.S. of $9.5 billion; that's a lot of happy pills being consumed. What this means is that a lot of people are dealing with their unhappiness in ways that will not lead to true happiness—you can't medicate your way to happiness, be it with drugs—prescription or recreational—or alcohol.

Babies and children are happy and joyous—a baby's laugh is infectious, because it is one that speaks of pure joy. Yet as the years progress and we become adults, we lose that sense of happiness and joy. All of a sudden we become burdened by the responsibilities of being an adult, and life then takes on a different meaning—and who then has the time to be happy? Spending time trying to be happy seems more like a frivolous pursuit.

Being happy is our birthright and part of our reason for living. If we can't be happy, what can we be? Ironically, even though the ability to be joyful and happy is second nature when we are young, as adults it has to become a learned skill.

Matthieu Ricard is a French academic turned Buddhist monk, and is the author of the 2006 bestseller, *Happiness: A Guide to Developing Life's Most Important Skill*. He has been called "the happiest person in the world," and believes the mind can be trained to be happy. "The mind is malleable," says Matthieu Ricard. "Our life can be greatly transformed by even a minimal change in how we manage our thoughts and perceive and interpret the world. Happiness is a skill. It requires effort and time."

What Ricard is saying is that your mind can rise above the stresses of living to increase your ability to be happy. As a monk and long-time meditator, Ricard has taken part in studies to show that meditating can cause overwhelming changes in levels of happiness.

MRI scans showed that he and other long-term meditators—who had completed more than 10,000 hours each—experienced a huge level of positive emotions in the left pre-frontal cortex of the brain, which is associated with happiness. The right-hand side, which handles negative thoughts, is suppressed.

Further studies have shown that even novices who have done only a little meditation have increased levels of happiness.

About being called "the happiest person in the world," Ricard says this:

> I usually reply that anyone can be the happiest man or woman in the world, provided he or she looks for happiness in the right place. Authentic happiness can only come from the long-term cultivation of wisdom, altruism, and compassion, and

from the complete eradication of mental toxins, such as hatred, attachment, and ignorance.

Sounds like a recipe for living a Low Density Lifestyle, and for not living a High Density one.

24

Better Relationships, Better Sex

I am getting nowhere with you and I can't let you go and I can't get through. – Ani Difranco

Sex is always about emotions. Good sex is about free emotions; bad sex is about blocked emotions. – Deepak Chopra

Love is the answer, but while you are waiting for the answer, sex raises some pretty good questions. – Woody Allen

Relationships, love and sex are complicated topics, full of pitfalls and entanglements, mishaps and risks, and also much bliss and happiness.

It's the arena in which we can become most vulnerable, in which our deepest intimacies can become known; it can also be the arena in which our buttons are pushed to the max.

It is a risk to enter into a relationship with another, to fall in love, and to have sexual relations, because the heart is the most fragile of organs.

Many a person has fallen in love only to have their heart broken, and then to swear off ever being in love again; they put a shield around their heart, and enclose it so that it becomes difficult for them to easily feel again.

Being in a relationship and in love is when you are challenged to be the most brutally honest, because it is when another touches your heart and soul. You are then forced to either get in touch with your own deepest feelings, or else run away and bury those feelings deep down within.

Everyone wants to be loved, but you also need to know how to love. It takes opening your heart, authenticity, the ability to communicate, compassion, tenderness, understanding, the letting down of your guard, the lessening of expectations, and the ability to be humble and not let your ego take control.

In other words, this love thing is a tall order. Many books exist on the subject, but even the experts are not always expert. That's because getting the love thing down can be complicated.

Life is messy, full of chaos and unpredictability, and so even the best of relationships can be messy. The map of the human heart has many roadblocks and detours along the way.

The more of a Low Density Lifestyle you live, the better your chances of finding a lasting relationship, especially if it is with another person who also lives that way. That is because when two people come together who both live a Low Density Lifestyle, there is a sense of calm and inner peace already within the relationship, leading to less potential for possible friction that can cause problems.

Now, you can work on yourself till the cows come home, but the real test comes when you're in a relationship, when love comes knocking on your door, and when you have the closest and most intimate of all encounters, the experience of sex, because this is when we are fully tested.

Sex, especially, is a subject that is often considered taboo and not to be talked about in polite circles. Granted, you don't want to be shouting off a rooftop about your sex life, nor is it necessary to talk about it with everyone you meet. After all, it is a personal matter.

But we are a sexually repressed culture, afraid to fully express our primal needs and enjoy the full pleasures of sex. But it shouldn't be that way. After all, it is the most natural of acts.

Again, the more of a Low Density Lifestyle you lead, the better your sex life can be.

When you are living a Low Density Lifestyle, you are naturally attracted to other people who are also living a Low Density Lifestyle, and it is these people who will make up your most intimate social network. If you feel centered, balanced and in the flow, you won't readily enjoy the company of people who live a completely opposite lifestyle, as it will just be too jarring to your soul.

Interestingly though, people who live a High Density Lifestyle will be naturally attracted to those who live a Low Density Lifestyle, because the calmness and peacefulness of someone living a Low Density Lifestyle is something that can help to balance and center someone living a High Density Lifestyle. It can actually be a profoundly transformative experience if someone living a High Density Lifestyle allows themselves to open up to the energies and calming influence of someone living a Low Density Lifestyle. So this is truly one case of opposites attracting!

But the tricky thing is that for those living a Low Density Lifestyle, the desire is to have happy and harmonious relationships, and they will go out of their way to find them and to reject relationships that create unhappiness and disharmony. So it's not impossible for people on opposite ends of the spectrums to come together—after all, the chemical bond of love transcends all boundaries and overcomes all limitations—it's just that if you want to have a sustaining and lasting relationship, there needs to be a bonding of two souls, one in which each person can gaze into the other's eyes and see the reflection of the deep and infinite waters of the Zero-Point Field, which is the origins of universal love and consciousness.

Communication is a big part of a relationship, and failure to communicate is a major reason for breakups. To be able to communicate, each party in a relationship needs to feel loved and safe. Each person in the relationship also has to let go of expectations and not judge or criticize the other, but instead help them to feel comfortable being able to communicate. Communicating your deepest and most intimate thoughts is not easy, but if you feel safe and loved, and feel that what you say won't be held against you, then it is easier to speak from your heart. This happens easier when both people in the relationship are living a Low Density Lifestyle.

If one or both people in the relationship are living a High Density Lifestyle, then it's a lot harder, because there's no feeling of safety in expressing intimate thoughts. These are the relationships that are doomed to fail.

Another important part of a strong and lasting relationship is the sex life. Because those living a Low Density Lifestyle are healthier and more balanced, less stressed and more in the flow, they have the capability of having a strong sex drive and having better sex. They understand that sexual desire is a natural biological urge, as opposed to a feeling that one should be ashamed of or should repress. They know that sex, and orgasm, make both parties feel good and is a vital part of making love. In addition, sex allows for intimacy and expressions of love, and these are things cherished by those living a Low Density Lifestyle.

For many people living a High Density Lifestyle, the only time when they're able to relax and feel comfortable having sex is when they imbibe in alcohol or recreational drugs, because these allow them to relax their inhibitions and feel less stressed.

Although sex can be very enjoyable when performed in an altered state, an important part of the sexual experience is the feeling of intimacy that one person has with another, because in that state of intimacy, a strong bond is formed between both people and the flow of love, happiness and joy circulates and is expressed between them. When a person is having sex in an altered state, the flow is impeded. But unfortunately, for many people living a High Density Lifestyle, having sex while in an altered state is the only way they can get full enjoyment of the act of making love.

Another great aspect of sex is that it increases your chances to be healthier and happier. People who have a regular sex life have been found to have a decreased risk of heart disease and stroke, a decrease of pain in the body, and an increase in life span. These are enormous motives for having a healthy sex life, but the reality is that in order to have a healthy and happy sex life, it is important that both people involved live a Low Density Lifestyle.

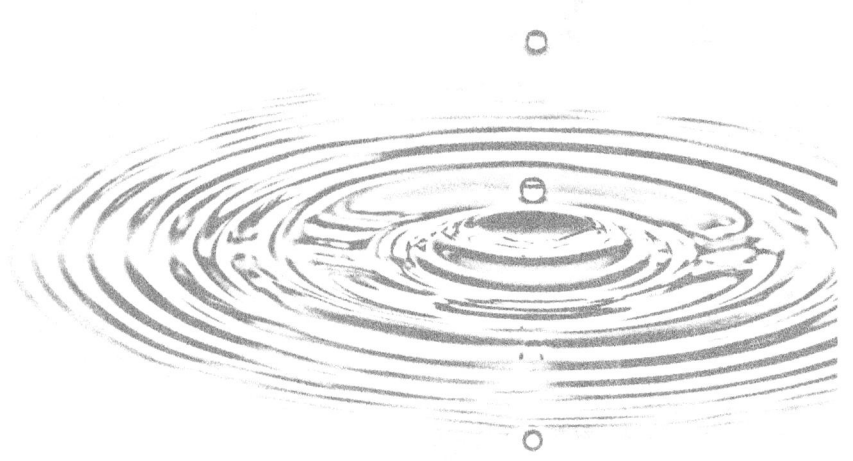

25

Focus and Clarity of Thought

Your vision will become clear only when you look into your heart.
- Carl Jung

To keep the body in good health is a duty, otherwise we shall not be able to keep our mind strong and clear. - Buddha

It is not enough to have a good mind. The main thing is to use it well.
- Rene Descartes

By feeling healthier; by being more clear with your attitude and emotions; and by becoming more mindful, more aware and more present in the body: if you are living a Low Density Lifestyle, you will be able to be more focused and have more clarity of thought.

The most optimal way to think is when you are relaxed and centered, because your thought processes will flow better. When you are stressed, your thought processes are scattered, and it's much harder to be focused.

That is why the worst thing you can do for yourself if you have a job that you have to do a lot of mind work, or you are in school and you do a lot of studying, is drink coffee. Even though it keeps you up and pumps adrenaline through your veins, making you feel like your thinking is more keen and focused, in actuality it causes you to be less focused, because all that adrenaline moving through your system stresses your body and mind, ultimately leaving you more scattered.

When you are more calm, relaxed and centered, and more focused and clear of thought, you are more fluid and flexible of body and mind and your brain can function at a more optimal capacity.

The brain produces different electrical frequencies, which can change over the course of a day, depending on what you are doing. The different brain states are delta waves, which are very slow waves and are produced during deep sleep; theta waves, which occur in the time between waking and sleeping, and is a wave that allows for experiencing a more vivid reality; alpha waves, which are produced when a person is meditating or in a state of deep relaxation; beta waves, which occur when a person is active and focusing on their work; and gamma waves, which is a frequency that is produced when a person is in a state of intensive learning.

All of these brain waves are important for functioning. The best scenario for optimal functioning of the mind is to be able to shift from one brain wave state to the other fluidly, flexibly and without impedance—in this situation, you will be more capable of focusing intently and experiencing a profound clarity of thought, because the brain waves are able to adapt easily and change readily according to each circumstance that presents itself.

You wouldn't want to necessarily be in a beta or gamma wave state when you're trying to sleep or relax, nor would you want to be producing delta or theta waves when you need to be fully alert.

— FOCUS AND CLARITY OF THOUGHT —

When you overtax your system because of being overstressed, or eating a poor diet, or being caught up in another of the impediments to living a Low Density Lifestyle, the brain loses the elasticity to shift between brain wave states, and you will suffer from a lack of focus and an inability to have clarity of thought. When you are like this, your brain becomes scrambled, so to speak—it's hard to focus, to think calmly and clearly.

If you are like this, you will act out, becoming impulsive and irrational. That is why when you live a High Density Lifestyle, it is hard to see clearly, and you suffer from a lack of clarity of thought.

26

Creativity and Genius

Straight-away the ideas flow in upon me, directly from God, and not only do I see distinct themes in my mind's eye, but they are clothed in the right forms, harmonies, and orchestration. – Johannes Brahms

Whenever an answer, a solution, or a creative idea is needed, stop thinking for a moment by focusing attention on your inner energy field.... When you resume thinking, it will be fresh and creative.
– Eckhart Tolle

You can't use up creativity, creative thinking builds on itself and increases the creativity of the thinker...You can't use up creativity. The more you use, the more you have. – Maya Angelou

As I discussed in Chapter 13, The Dreamer, using the imagination and creative thinking abilities is an essential part of living a Low Density Lifestyle. When you are in the flow and using these capabilities, you are able to access the Zero-Point Field, which is the portal of the universe that all energy and matter emanate from, and is also the source point of consciousness and information.

This is also the source of creativity and creative thinking. Creativity researchers looking into the source of ideas have found that most ideas come to people in dreams—night or day—in reveries, or in some other inexplicable manner. The truth is that most of these ideas come from the Zero-Point Field.

High densities in the body impede your ability to pick up the frequencies and signals that derive from the Zero-Point Field, making it that much harder for people in a High Density Lifestyle to fully use their mind's greater potential.

On the other hand, folks living a Low Density Lifestyle are more proficient at using their mind's greater potential, and feeling more fulfilled in general, because they are able to tap into their innate creative powers.

Another beneficial aspect of using more of the mind's potential is being able to tap into your own inner genius. Everyone has the ability to think, act, perform and execute at peak performance levels, but it only truly occurs when you are functioning at an optimal level. When you use more of your innate potential it means you are operating at a much higher level—a Low Density level—than most other people.

If you live your life in this way you are fully capable of inspiring others to reach for the stars and also live this way.

One of the barometers, in some circles, for whether a person will be successful is their IQ. The higher the IQ, the more intelligent someone is and supposedly the more successful they will be.

Daniel Goleman, in his book *Emotional Intelligence: Why It Can Matter More Than IQ*, demonstrated that IQ does not predict how successful a person will be in life. Instead he showed that a person's emotional intelligence, their ability to act in a mature and well-adjusted way in social situations, and manage the emotions of one's self, of others and of groups, is a better measure of success.

In addition to emotional intelligence, I think another measure of success is a person's DQ—their Density Intelligence. A person's DQ, or

— CREATIVITY AND GENIUS —

Density Intelligence, may be the biggest indicator of how happy, healthy and fulfilled they are. What Density Intelligence shows is how flexible, creative and curious a person's thinking habits are; or how rigid, tense and inflexible those thinking habits are.

A person with low Density Intelligence is someone who is able to see in more interconnected and holistic ways, because their thinking is less dense and more flexible; a person with high Density Intelligence will be more stubborn and dogmatic because their thinking is more dense, or rigid.

To cultivate low Density Intelligence, and therefore use more of your mind's potential and your innate inner genius, here are 10 things for you to put into practice:

1. Mindfulness – Do you know who you really are? How much of the time are you present and fully aware?

2. Idealism – Are you an idealist and someone who prefers to live a principled life?

3. The Capacity to Face and Use Adversity – We all make mistakes and we all face adversity. Do you own your mistakes and use adversity and the pain that goes with it to learn?

4. Being Holistic – Do you see the interconnections between everything?

5. Being Open – Are you open to new ideas, to things that are different? Or do you just have a knee-jerk reaction when something comes your way that is not the same-old, same-old?

6. Thinking with Head and Heart – Do you integrate critical thinking with what your heart tells you? In other words, do you think with both your head and heart?

7. Courage – Do you have the courage to be independent, to not do what is expedient or what the group wants you to do? Are you willing to stand on your own two feet for what you believe in, and to do the right thing?

8. Asking Questions – Do you take things at face value or do you want to know more, and to get at the heart of the matter, in order to form your own opinion and to think for yourself?

9. Re-Framing Ideas – Do you take things you are presented with and put it into a larger context of meaning, something that has practical value for you and others?

10. Spontaneity – Do you make decisions and react to things based on fear, so that you have an immediate and negative knee-jerk reaction? Or are your responses based on the situation at hand, so that your response is appropriate to the situation?

27

Productivity and Success

Life's irony is that as soon as worldly goods and worldly success are of no concern to you, the way is open for them to flow to you.
- Neal Donald Walsch

I honestly think it is better to be a failure at something you love than to be a success at something you hate. - George Burns

Is not life a hundred times too short for us to bore ourselves?
- Friedrich Nietzsche

The most productive and successful people are those who are doing what they love. They work hard, usually much harder than others, but they do it with effortless effort. Work doesn't seem like work at all; instead it's like play. They are able to get by on less sleep and still produce more.

In the field of economics, the study of productivity and increasing worker efficiency has produced reams of papers, books and doctoral theses. The focus of these is usually on how to generate an improvement in labor efficiency per unit of time. Ideas on developing enhanced employee output run the gamut from more automation of repetitive tasks, to increasing worker comfort with better ergonomic design, raising workplace temperature, and perfuming or deodorizing the air conditioning system.

But there is really only one way for employees to be more productive: they need to be happy, fulfilled by their work and feel like they have a sense of purpose. In other words, within the confines of the workplace, they must be doing something that they love. For this to happen, they need to be guided towards a Low Density Lifestyle.

And for people who are not employees, who tend towards the entrepreneurial, then it's even more imperative that the work you do is work you love. You have to, as Joseph Campbell says, "Follow your bliss." Perhaps when you do so things won't work out as planned, but invariably as one door closes another door opens. In other words, if you try, good things will happen, but if you never try, nothing will happen.

As Oprah Winfrey has said, "Do the one thing you think you cannot do. Fail at it. Try again. Do better the second time. The only people who never tumble are those who never mount the high wire. This is your moment. Own it."

To be more productive, one of the best tips is based on a story about the early 20th century industrialist, J. P. Morgan. The story goes that one day in the early 1900s a stranger approached Morgan as he walked down a street in New York City. Holding up an envelope, the man said, "Sir, in my hand I hold a guaranteed formula for success, which I will gladly sell you for $25,000."

"Sir," Morgan replied, "I do not know what is in that envelope. However, if you show me, and I like what I see, I give you my word as a gentleman that I will pay what you ask."

The man thought about it, agreed to Morgan's terms, and handed over the envelope. Without pause, Morgan opened the envelope, pulled out a single sheet of paper, unfolded it, and gave it a quick glance. He thereupon handed the paper and envelope back to the stranger.

And then he reached a hand into his overcoat, pulled out his checkbook, and wrote a check for $25,000. The paper read:

> 1. Every morning, write a list of the things that need to be done that day.
> 2. Do them.

The more productive you are, the better your chances of success. But what exactly is success? Henry David Thoreau once said, "I have learned that if one advances confidently in the direction of his dreams, and endeavors to live the life he has imagined, he will meet with a success unexpected in common hours."

For people living a Low Density Lifestyle, success is part of their biochemical makeup because they are willing to dream, imagine and use their inner genius, and to then make those aspirations a reality.

Success can be measured in many ways: for some it is attaining a certain amount of money, while for others it is the ability to do good and have an impact on others, to live a principled life in which sound judgment is continually utilized, to reach a goal that seemed insurmountable, or to live a fulfilled life full of passion and joy.

The ultimate definition of success—the Low Density Lifestyle definition—is attaining a dream, something that you have set out to do, while at the same time being able to sleep peacefully at night, because you know that in reaching the goal, you did it with integrity, honor and doing no harm to others.

It may take longer to achieve goals in this way, but folks who realize success in this way realize that ultimately, the journey is the destination, and the path is a process that offers much to learn, experience, savor and gain wisdom from.

As the author Stephen King said,

> Do you do it for the money, honey? The answer is no. Don't now and never did. Yes, I've made a great deal of dough from my fiction, but I never set a single word down on paper with the thought of being paid for it... I have written because it fulfilled me. Maybe it paid off the mortgage on the house and got the kids through college, but those things were on the side—I did it for the buzz. I did it for the pure joy of the thing. And if you can do it for joy, you can do it forever.

28

Intuition

By banishing doubt and trusting your intuitive feelings, you clear a space for the power of intention to flow through.
- Wayne Dyer

If a man does not keep pace with his companions, perhaps it is because he hears a different drummer. Let him step to the music which he hears, however measured or far away.
- Henry David Thoreau

You have to leave the city of your comfort and go into the wilderness of your intuition. What you'll discover will be wonderful. What you'll discover is yourself. - Alan Alda

Intuition is, by definition, a non-rational means of knowing. The word intuition comes from the Latin word "intueri," which is often roughly translated as meaning "to look inside" or "to contemplate." Intuitive insight is something that comes in a flash, and something that occurs outside the realm of reason. A person has a gut feeling, something they just know to be true, and yet it can't be quantified. Everyone has intuitive capabilities, but not everyone is willing to trust their intuition.

People who live a High Density Lifestyle generally don't trust their feelings, because they tend to be overly analytical and somewhat rigid of thinking. The 17th century mathematician and philosopher Blaise Pascal said, "There are two types of mind... the mathematical, and what might be called the intuitive. The former arrives at its views slowly, but they are firm and rigid; the latter is endowed with greater flexibility and applies itself simultaneously to the diverse lovable parts of that which it loves."

Some scientists have contended that intuition is associated with innovation in scientific discovery. Jonas Salk, a scientist who valued intuition, once wrote "the intuitive mind tells the thinking mind where to look."

And Albert Einstein, who was a highly intuitive scientist, said, "the workings of intuition transcend those of the intellect, and as is well known, innovation is often a triumph of intuition over logic."

Because we live in a predominantly High Density Lifestyle world, we have learned to value reason over intuition. That's not to say that we should throw out reason and only use intuition; instead there's room for both. It should be that we integrate the two and form our decisions with both head and heart.

People who live a Low Density Lifestyle can more readily access their intuitive powers and have a more acute intuitive sense about things. When a person experiences more flow in their life, they have fewer densities in their body that block the signals and frequencies that emanate from the Zero-Point Field. The ability to pick up the signals of the Zero-Point Field is what is called intuition; it is a gift that anyone who lives a life of abundance has, because they are one with the Universal Flow.

29

Inner Peace

Better indeed is knowledge than mechanical practice. Better than knowledge is meditation. But better still is surrender of attachment to results, because there follows immediate peace. — Bhagavad Gita

If you scramble about in search of inner peace, you will lose your inner peace. - Lao Tzu

Real peace is not in power, money, or weapons, but in deep inner peace.
- Thich Nhat Hanh

Inner peace is a condition easily known and attained by people living a Low Density Lifestyle—it truly is second nature because they are used to experiencing stillness, quiet and calm.

Inner peace is a state of being where you are mentally and spiritually at peace, and those who embody it are capable of staying balanced and centered even when they are faced with discord or stress; their disposition is one that is free from the effects of stress. When you are at peace with yourself, you are capable of living a life with much joy, happiness and integrity—that is because you have a sense of being connected to the spiritual dimension of life.

There are many approaches to achieving inner peace: prayer, meditation, yoga, tai chi and being in nature are just a few. When you find inner peace, you then are on the path of truly knowing yourself.

Inner peace is not just something that has merit for an individual; it is the ultimate path for peace in our world. As His Holiness the Dalai Lama says:

> Responsibility does not only lie with the leaders of our countries or with those who have been appointed or elected to do a particular job. It lies with each of us individually. Peace, for example, starts within each one of us. When we have inner peace, we can be at peace with those around us.

The country of Bhutan is known as "the happiest country in the world." Situated in the Himalayan Mountains between India and China, they are a Buddhist nation, and a highly spiritual nation.

Bhutan has made sure that happiness is part of their economic and political system, by measuring their country's success not by a Gross National Product by instead a Gross Happiness Product.

Under the Bhutan Constitution, government programs—from agriculture to transportation to foreign trade—must be judged not by the economic benefits they may offer but by the happiness—the Gross National Happiness—they produce.

How did a country develop such a philosophy? By being a country that places a premium on inner peace as a core principle of living, they have seen to it that a superior quality of life is the primary need and want of the population.

30

Enlightenment

Knowing others is wisdom, knowing yourself is Enlightenment.
— Lao Tzu

Spirituality is a domain of awareness. — Deepak Chopra

We have always been involved in spiritual evolution.
We are spiritual beings, we have always been spiritual beings
and we will always be spiritual beings. — Gary Zukav

Enlightenment is the sum total of putting into action all the twelve steps outlined in Part II of this book.

But what is enlightenment? In a broad sense, enlightenment means wisdom or a clarity of perception. In 1784, the philosopher Immanuel Kant wrote a famous essay entitled "What is Enlightenment?" in which he attempted to answer the question.

"Enlightenment is man's emergence from his self-incurred immaturity," Kant began the essay, and continued on for another 2,600 words. The gist of what Kant said is that immaturity is self-inflicted not from a lack of understanding, but from the lack of courage to use one's reason, intellect, and wisdom without the guidance of another. It is "our fear of thinking for ourselves," he proclaimed, and he exhorted the reader of his essay to "Sapere aude!": Dare to be wise.

Enlightenment is a life of wisdom, knowledge, insight and clarity of thought. It is about functioning at peak capability, of feeling interconnected with all facets of the universe, and of understanding on a profound level how the universe operates. A person who is enlightened is also FREE: they are in the flow, they embody relaxation, calmness and stillness, and they act with effortless effort.

A person who is enlightened is also awakened from the veil of illusion, what in Hinduism is called Maya.

In theories of enlightenment, it is understood that humans go through an evolution of consciousness, and the more enlightened a person becomes in their lifetime, the higher up the evolutionary ladder of consciousness do they go. According to this, these people are capable of thinking more holistically and truly understanding the integral connection between the world of science and matter and the world of spirit.

Some of the people who experience enlightenment in this way become leaders in their community or in the greater society, while others keep a lower profile and prefer a quiet, peaceful existence; nevertheless, all of these people are teachers in one way or another. And all of these people live (or have lived) a Low Density Lifestyle.

Conclusion: Being Bold, Touching Your Greatness

For better or for worse, our future is now closely tied to human creativity. The result will be determined in large part by our dreams and by the struggle to make them real.
— Mihaly Csikszentmihalyi

And as we let our own light shine, we unconsciously give other people permission to do the same. As we are liberated from our fear, our presence automatically liberates others.
— Marianne Williamson

Boldness has genius, power, and magic in it. Begin it now.
— Johann Wolfgang Von Goethe

As you venture forward in the realm of a Low Density Lifestyle, you will find yourself living your life to your peak potential, and because of that you will have the ability to touch your greatness. When you are healthy; happy; doing what you love; feeling fulfilled; and utilizing your creative intelligence, innate genius and visionary potential; there is no limit to what you can accomplish.

You will also have the capacity to be bold with your vision of life and to inspire others. If there were more people living a Low Density Lifestyle and willing to be bold with their vision and inspire others, this world could experience a profound transformation.

In chapter 13, The Dreamer, I had a number of quotes from visionaries who understood this. Here is a repeat of three of them:

> **John F. Kennedy:** The problems of the world cannot possibly be solved by skeptics or cynics whose horizons are limited by the obvious realities. We need men who can dream of things that never were.
>
> **Robert F. Kennedy:** There are those who look at things the way they are, and ask why. I dream of things that never were, and ask why not?
>
> **Dalai Lama:** With realization of one's own potential and self-confidence in one's ability, one can build a better world.

If a majority of people lived a Low Density Lifestyle, or at least a sizeable minority, the world we live in would be a world of peace; a world of a sane health care system; a world where people help one another without thinking, what's in it for me; a world where people live their dream and answer to their calling; a world where people could overcome their fears and take bold action; a world where people didn't let things impede them from finding what it is that they loved to do; and a world of forward-thinking visionaries.

In other words, it would be one amazing and mighty world.

And it can start right now. You have it in your power to do so and

— CONCLUSION —

move things forward. Life is far too short to live a High Density Lifestyle, to be caught up in things that are draining your energy, your life, and your potential.

Move towards the positive, move towards the light, move towards using your full potential. Move towards living a Low Density Lifestyle.

As Marianne Williamson wrote in *A Return to Love: Reflections on the Principles of A Course in Miracles*:

> Our deepest fear is not that we are inadequate. Our deepest fear is that we are powerful beyond measure. It is our light, not our darkness, that frightens us most. We ask ourselves, "Who am I to be brilliant, gorgeous, talented, and famous?" Actually, who are you not to be? You are a child of God. Your playing small does not serve the world. There is nothing enlightened about shrinking so that people won't feel insecure around you. We were born to make manifest the glory of God that is within us. It's not just in some of us; it's in all of us. And when we let our own light shine, we unconsciously give other people permission to do the same. As we are liberated from our own fear, our presence automatically liberates others.

In each of us is a seed that is hungry to be sparked. It is the desire for meaning, to live a life that has profound value not only to you but also to others. This hunger cannot be quenched: it needs to be watered, fed, nurtured, cultivated, and finally allowed to blossom.

As it sprouts, it will call you, burn at you, demand from you. It will point you in the right direction. You cannot suppress it, because it cannot be squelched. Listen to it. It is the rivers of the pulse of the universe, the Zero-Point Field, calling your name.

It wants you to live a Low Density Lifestyle so that the communication that is directed to your soul will be heard by you.

We are all interconnected, all reflections of the celestial bodies of the greater universe, and all of us can hear this, if we allow ourselves to.

Answer the call, and you will touch your greatness.

About the Author

Michael Wayne, Ph.D., L.Ac., is the author of the groundbreaking book, *Quantum-Integral Medicine: Towards a New Science of Healing and Human Potential*. He also has written a novel, *The Knuckleball From Hell*.

He is the Founder and Director of The Center for Quantum Transformation. Dr. Wayne also has over 25 years experience in the field of Chinese Medicine, and has a private practice as an Acupuncturist and Chinese Herbalist.

Dr. Wayne's work has been publicly praised by Marianne Williamson and Dr. Larry Dossey; he has received national media attention and appeared in over 100 print publications, radio and TV shows, including *Alternative Medicine*, the *New York Post*, *Hay House Radio*, *Positive Health*, *Wellbeing Journal*, *MyTekLife*, and *Acupuncture Today*.

He has pioneered the Low-Density Lifestyle, a concept that addresses each aspect of a person's physical, emotional and spiritual health to free themselves of the behaviors that are weighing them down and limiting their potential.

The Low Density Lifestyle website is www.lowdensitylifestyle.com.

Dr. Wayne's website is www.drmichaelwayne.com.

www.ingramcontent.com/pod-product-compliance
Lightning Source LLC
Chambersburg PA
CBHW070801100426
42742CB00012B/2216